MW00941692

A STRATEGY ROUNDTABLE ON
DEMOCRATS AND THE WHITE WORKING CLASS

12 leading progressive political strategists present fact based proposals for regaining the trust of working Americans and winning their votes in the years ahead.

CONTRIBUTORS INCLUDE:

Stan Greenberg

Ruy Teixeira

Harold Meyerson

Karen Nussbaum

Guy Molyneux

Celinda Lake

Joan Walsh

Bob Kuttner

Ed Kilgore

Matt Morrison

Justin Gest

Andrew Levison

Co-sponsored by The American Prospect and the White Working Class Roundtable

Published by Democratic Strategist Press

Democrats and the White Working Class is the product of a collaboration between
The American Prospect and The White Working Class Roundtable.

The American Prospect, Founded in 1990, publishes print and digital editions
of the magazine four times a year. The online Prospect offers
additional coverage and commentary on a daily basis.
The Prospect can be found at www.prospect.org

The White Working Class Roundtable is a project of The Democratic Strategist.
Created in 2013, the project has conducted and published two major roundtable
discussions and issues a regular quarterly newsletter.
The Roundtable can be found online at
http://thedemocraticstrategist-roundtables.com/
The Democratic Strategist is available online at
www.thedemocraticstrategist.org.
Communications regarding the book can be sent to
editors@thedemcraticstrategist.org

DEDICATION

This book is sincerely dedicated to the scores of new progressive
candidates and the hundreds of door to door canvassers and grass-roots
organizers who will fan out across white working class neighborhoods
and communities in "Red State" America in the next few years, seeking to build a
renewed progressive and Democratic presence where
Democrats and progressives have been absent for far too long.

While this collection of articles strongly reflects the
contributors' firm belief that successful political strategies
to regain the trust and support of working Americans
must always be deeply grounded in the careful and methodical analysis
of hard data, it is our genuine hope that the ideas
it presents will be of direct practical use to the men and women in the field
and even a source of inspiration.

TABLE OF CONTENTS

WELCOME:

Facing the Challenge: Regaining the Trust and Winning Back the Support of the White Working Class Democrats and Independents Who Defected to Trump in 2016

Stanley Greenberg, Ruy Teixeira, Karen Nussbaum and Harold Meyerson

The four of us are among the founding members of the White Working Class Roundtable, a group which brings together political strategists and thinkers who seek to bridge the gap between progressives and the white working class. Early this Spring we four decided to join together to issue an invitation to a range of prominent individuals who have devoted their careers to studying white working class Americans and ask them to present their thoughts and recommendations for the future.

The twelve papers presented in this Roundtable discussion include data derived from a wide range of research methods—from opinion polls and focus groups to sociological field studies and data gathered from door to door political canvassing and grass-roots organizing. They propose a wide variety of specific strategies and approaches but they also agree on several basic ideas.

First, progressives and Democrats should focus on the "persuadable" sector of the white working class. Data from every research method and technique indicates that there are substantial numbers of white working class Trump voters who do not genuinely share Trump's bigotry and intolerance and who will become increasingly disillusioned as he betrays more and more of his populist campaign promises. The challenge for Democratic candidates will not be to change the minds of the substantial group of racists and bigots who are indeed among Trump's most committed supporters but rather to present a progressive alternative that the more tolerant men and women in white working class America can find genuinely convincing and believable.

Second, progressive candidates must not only offer populist economic proposals but also a firm commitment to profoundly reforming both government at every level and also the Democratic Party itself. White working Americans are not simply cynical about the role of big money in politics. They have also become convinced that government policies and programs invariably end up benefiting either the wealthy or the poor but never themselves. They also believe that Democrats have absolutely no commitment to serious reform of this corrupt system. Many white working Americans who might otherwise be "persuadable" will simply refuse to vote for Democrats until this perception is changed.

Third, progressives and Democrats must offer white working class Americans candidates who are committed to genuinely *representing* them and not simply to promising them a preselected platform of liberal programs and policies. The persuadable sector of the white working class does not need to be offered appeals to racism or other right-wing views but they must absolutely feel that a Democratic candidate seeking their vote will be their firm and passionate advocate—someone who will be deeply committed to understanding their real day-to-day problems and representing their *unique and specific needs and interests* in the political system. Donald Trump's most potent appeal to white working class voters was his charge that all of the other candidates did not even make a pretence of sincerely wanting to represent white workers while he, on the other hand, promised to be totally and exclusively "their man" and sincerely "on their side."

Fourth, progressives and Democrats must develop local, community-based political organizations in white working class America that are built from the bottom up not the top down. Massive advertising campaigns will not win back the support of white working class Americans, no matter how cleverly written or precisely targeted such ads may be. Door to door canvassing that only occurs during election seasons will not build solid and permanent support, no matter how energetic or committed the volunteers may be. The most influential political organizer is always the person who lives on the block or the neighbor next door. Trump appeared to have no formal political organization but in reality his candidacy was supported by the vast network of permanent grass roots conservative organizations that have deep neighborhood-level roots in white working class communities—the Tea Party, The NRA, pro-life groups and other organizations of the religious right.

Finally, progressive campaigns and candidates must be committed to learning from experience. Many different progressive and Democratic groups will be running candidates and engaging in extensive voter mobilization in 2018 and 2020. They will follow a range of strategies and offer a range of different kinds of appeals in white working class communities. Progressives and Democrats must be firmly dedicated to studying every one of these campaigns honestly and objectively, learning the lessons from their various successes and failures.

These recommendations do not offer a prescription for a quick reversal of the massive loss of white working class support progressives and Democrats suffered last year. But the simple fact is that no such quick solution is possible. We believe that progressives and Democrats can indeed regain the trust and win back the votes of the many white working Americans who have increasingly abandoned the Democratic Party but only through a hard and dedicated work that lasts for years. The reality must be faced. There is no other way.

INTRODUCTION:
The White Working Class: An American Dilemma
Harold Meyerson

Harold Meyerson is the
Executive Editor of
The American Prospect

With our partners at The Democratic Strategist, *The American Prospect* is co-publishing this series of articles on one of the most contentious topics in today's political discourse, and one of progressives' and the Democratic Party's most vexing problems: the white working class.

The need for such a discussion is both obvious and two-fold. First, the white working class—the bedrock of the long-vanished New Deal Coalition—has largely and increasingly been abandoning the Democratic Party, even when that has meant voting against some of its economic interests. While Hillary Clinton's loss of such presumably blue-wall states as Wisconsin, Michigan and Pennsylvania dramatized the extent of the Democrats' problem, it was also just the latest stage of an epochal shift. Wisconsin, after all, has a wall-to-wall reactionary state government, with Scott Walker having won three elections placing and then keeping him in the governor's office. Michigan also has a Republican governor and Republican control of both houses of the legislature, while in Pennsylvania, Republicans control the legislative branch as well.

Second, every economic and public-health index of how Americans are faring has been turning up alarming news about the white working class during the past several years—a cascade of data showing how their incomes, employment opportunities and labor force participation have been falling, while their rates of drug, alcohol and opioid abuse have been rising, and their very lifespans have been growing shorter.

Nonetheless, some in the Democratic camp argue that the party can win without making any special overtures to white workers. The premises behind these arguments, however, are shaky at best. The first premise is that the Rising American Electorate of minorities, women (especially unmarried women), millennials and increasing numbers of professionals (especially those with post-graduate degrees) is sufficient in itself to win elections.

Several of the articles in this package, by the very pollsters, demographers and analysts who coined and popularized the notion of the Rising American Electorate, dispel that premise, however. Most prominently, the article by Ruy Teixeira, John Halpin and Robert Griffin points out that winning control of the House of Representatives becomes very difficult absent a respectable Democratic performance (which needn't mean a majority) among white working class voters. As they document:

> [F]or the purposes of political representation one would be hard pressed to name a group—past, present, or future—that is better spread out than the white working class. As a single data point, consider the following: while 43 percent of the age 25-or-older population in the United States is WWC, the median congressional district is just a little over 60 percent WWC…. Only 26 percent of congressional districts have age 25+ populations that are less than half WWC, a striking disparity given the nation's overall composition.

And that's just the House. Winning control of the Senate, not to mention winning the 60 seats still needed to pass major legislation there, wil require Democrats to ring up victories in states where the white working class will loom large numerically for some time to come. That includes most of the states of the post-industrial Midwest, to which immigrants have not been flocking precisely because of the limited economic opportunities those states have to offer.

Moreover, as Ed Kilgore points out in his article, if the Democrats don't win enough white working class votes to retake some of the state legislatures they've lost in recent years, the next decennial redistricting could lock in Republican dominance at the state and national level for yet another decade.

The second premise of the argument opposed to the Democrats' making a major effort to do better among white working class voters is that it's a hopeless cause: that they're either so ideologically conservative or so culturally estranged from today's progressives and Democrats that it would be a wasted investment. But as pollster Guy Molyneux documented in the Winter 2016 issue of the *Prospect* [http://prospect.org/article/mapping-white-working-class] and as Andrew Levison and the authors of the Working America survey demonstrate in this package of articles, the white working class not only contains its share of progressives, but also, and crucially, a bloc of swing voters that is not ideologically conservative on economic questions and not so estranged from the Democrats on cultural issues that they constitute a lost cause when Democratic candidates and progressive canvassers come calling. That bloc, these authors show, is large enough to produce Democratic victories—if and when, and with what policies and candidates, Democrats know how to reach out to them.

The third premise of why the Democrats shouldn't reach out to white working class voters is that it will compel Democrats to jettison positions—some of their support for minority rights, cultural liberalism and climate change mitigation—that have become much of the ideological bedrock of contemporary progressivism and today's Democratic Party. To this, our contributors offer a range of counter arguments. Pollsters Stan Greenberg and Celinda Lake demonstrate how a more aggressive and substantive economic populism not only will win the allegiance of swing white working class voters but increase Democratic margins among minority voters as well. Greenberg and Guy Molyneux caution, however, that progressives must also tap into the anger against political elites, whom white working class voters (and lots of other folks, too) see as favoring the interests of the wealthy and corporations over those of their own constituents. Andy Levison argues that Democrats need to entertain a degree of cultural pluralism when mounting candidacies in predominantly white working class districts, while still adhering to the party's culturally progressive norms nationally.

A cautionary note is sounded by Joan Walsh, who argues that all the economic populism in the world may not help the Democrats win the votes of many within the white working class whose racism and sexism present insuperable barriers to building progressive or Democratic majorities. Walsh doesn't reject the substance of a pro-working class economics—but that's because she believes these are policies the nation needs to embrace, not because she holds out much hope that they'll sway many white working class voters.

Something of a counterargument to Walsh's is presented by Jason Gest, who explains how statewide Democratic candidates, including Governor Steve Bullock, keep winning in Montana even though it's overwhelmingly a white working class state, and one that went heavily for Trump. Like Levison, Bullock writes that candidates who embody their constituency's cultural values are a *sine qua non* for electoral victory. He acknowledges that finding a candidate who can do that nationally—finding candidates who can embody the culture of Montana ranchers and, say, theater-industry workers on Manhattan's Upper West Side—is an impossibility. What a national candidate can do, he concludes, is acknowledge the legitimacy of various cultures, and stress the common economic interests of such diverse groups by battling the financial and corporate elites that have stripped those groups of both income and power.

My own prescription for what progressives and Democrats need to do to perform better among white working class voters is geographic, regional, and long-term. It begins with understanding just how profoundly most regions of the country have been left behind by our new high-tech economy.

In May of 2016, the Economic Innovation Group released a study—"The New Map of Economic Growth and Recovery" [http://eig.org/wp-content/uploads/2016/05/recoverygrowthreport.pdf]—that made no discernible impact on progressive discourse or Democrats' strategy during that year's campaigns. But, like the Angus Deaton-Ann Case studies on rising death rates within the white working class—which did enter progressive discourse but also had no impact on Democrats' strategy—it sure as hell should have.

The EIG's study strikes me as the necessary corollary to the Deaton-Case documentation of the rise in "deaths of despair." What it shows, simply, is that businesses and employment opportunities are concentrated as never before in a shrinking number of metropolises, and that the economies of Everyplace Else in America are hollowing out.

Consider these stark numbers: In the economic recovery of 1992-1996, the share of new business establishments created in counties with fewer than 100,000 residents was 32 percent; in counties of 100,000 to 500,000 residents, 39 percent; and in counties with more than one million residents 13 percent. In the economic recovery of 2002-2006, the share of new businesses in counties with fewer than 100,000 was 15 percent; in counties of 100,000 to 500,000, 36 percent; and in counties with more than one million, 29 percent. In the 2010-2014 recovery, the share of new business in counties with fewer than 100,000 was zero percent; in counties between 100,000 and 500,000, 23 percent; and in counties with more than one million, 58 percent. In the recovery of 2010-2014, fully half of all new businesses were located in just 20 counties.

If you live outside the big cities, what's not to despair?

The geographic trend in net job creation, of course, tracks the trend in business creation. In the recovery of 1992-1996, counties with fewer than 100,000 residents accounted for 27 percent of the net increase in the nation's jobs. In the recovery of 2010-2014, they accounted for one-third of that—just 9 percent of the new jobs. Conversely, in the 1992-96 recovery, counties with more than one million residents accounted for just 16 percent of the new jobs created, while in the 2010-2014 recovery, they accounted for 41 percent.

It should come as no surprise, then, that when Working America surveyed the vote in five key swing states in the 2016 election—Florida, North Carolina, Ohio, Pennsylvania and Wisconsin—it found that the counties in which Hillary Clinton's share of the vote declined most from that of Barack Obama in 2012 were the states' rural counties. It also found that the economic metric that most set apart those counties from their urban counterparts in their respective states was labor force participation: the rates were far lower in rural areas than in major cities.

If the Clinton campaign didn't recognize these new metro-rural polarities, the Trump campaign clearly did. His message of job creation was plainly one that resonated in places where work had disappeared, and the rural locations of many of his campaign rallies in the weeks before the election, while bewildering much of the press corps, actually reflected very acute targeting.

So Step One for the Democrats in reclaiming a necessary share of the white working class vote is to recognize that their nation suffers from two geographically distinct kinds of economic underdevelopment. One is the kind common to those otherwise prosperous urban areas, where millions of predominantly minority Americans labor in low-wage service and retail jobs. This species of underdevelopment is one with which Democrats are familiar and, indeed, have sought to redress with higher minimum wages, paid sick day and enhanced overtime regulations, and (completely unsuccessfully) labor law reform.

But the Democrats have failed even to recognize the second kind of underdevelopment, which is that now plaguing non-metropolitan America, a land of decaying factories, abandoned mill towns and depopulated farms. Or, less apocalyptically, small cities and towns struggling to get by. Raising the minimum wage is good in itself, but doesn't do much for a town where work opportunities have all but vanished.

Step Two in the Democrats' white working class quest is to recognize that market forces in themselves won't revive America's abandoned midlands—indeed, that they're responsible for that abandonment—and that the Democrats can draw on their own history of using government to develop underdeveloped regions. That's the essence of Jordan Schwarz's brilliant and largely forgotten 1993 history of the New Deal, entitled, rather dully, *The New Dealers*. Schwarz demonstrates that one central focus of Roosevelt's presidency was to invest in public works that would help raise the economies of the South and the West to nearer the national norm, through the Tennessee Valley Authority, a host of hydroelectric mega-projects in the West, and the Rural Electrification Administration; through financial reforms that strengthened regional banks and held Wall Street in check; and through public jobs projects like the WPA. In the wake of the downturn of 1937-1938 (induced by Roosevelt's attempt to cut spending to balance the budget—in a nation still suffering from double-digit unemployment), New Dealers like Jerome Frank and Beardsley Ruml floated such ideas as regional investment banks to bolster particularly hard-hit parts of the country. Their idea went nowhere, but defens spending in the build-up to World War II rode to the nation's economic rescue. And straight through the end of the Cold War, the arms economy served as the nation's public investment/economic development program. Presidents got their Pentagon budgets approved by members of Congress who insisted on defense plants in their districts, while the Reagan Administration in particular made a special point of directing that spending to their electoral base in Sunbelt states. But the Cold War's end brought with it an end to the military Keyensianism that had propped up much of the nation's economy, most especially in non-metropolitan areas. The niche conflicts that engage the Pentagon today don't require that level of manufacturing (nor does today's semi-robotized manufacturing require as many people as it used to).

Step Three in the Democrats' political revival, then, is to develop and promote a new regional revival strategy—and the "region" is really non-metropolitan America. With manufacturing employing a steadily smaller share of the nation's work force, that's not an easy challenge. And the kind of instant mass employment created by the WPA—most of whose workers used picks and shovels—can't easily be recreated today, either.

But that doesn't mean the Democrats' hands are tied. For starters, the Democrats should support not simply more infrastructure spending, but specific infrastructure development plans for every state, and an infrastructure bank, or a system of regional infrastructure banks, that could fund them. In the 1970s and '80s, Californians were presented with ballot measures that would authorize public bonding to create infrastructure projects; they almost always failed. Once the authors of such proposals wised up and began promoting ballot measures that specified which highways would be built where, and which upgraded, and which districts would get more schools and more parks, the ballot measures began to pass. This is not to say that the national Democrats need to get that specific, of course, but it would be a good idea to develop outlines for plans in each of the 50 states. Those plans could also include, as Vox editor and Prospect alum Matt Yglesias has suggested, relocating agencies of the federal government to different parts of the country, and finding ways to incentivize corporations to move operations outside the nation's mega-cities.

If the Democrats need a 50-state political strategy, they need to pair it up with a 50-state economic strategy.

Many of the party's existing economic plans play well in both spheres of underdevelopment, the urban and the rural, and among groups found in both places, such as millennials. Reducing costs and/or eliminating tuition at public colleges and universities is popular everywhere. The public's level of support for Medicaid, which Paul Ryan's proposed ACA repeal sought to slash, is overwhelming: a Quinnipiac Poll from March found just 22 percent favored cuts while 74 percent opposed them; among white working class respondents, 29 percent favored the cuts and 66 percent didn't. The declining incomes of white workers and the rising eligibility thresholds of the ACA have combined to de-stigmatize Medicaid in ways that Ryan and his ilk failed to anticipate.

But just as Democrats speak to preponderantly urban and largely minority service sector workers not just with national programs but also with their support for raising the local minimum wage and kindred measures, they need to speak to preponderantly non-metropolitan and largely white working class voters with policies for non-metropolitan development and job creation. Donald Trump won the White House on vague promises to do that, fool's gold though they'll turn out to be.

Now, the Democrats need to deliver the real thing.

They did once. In 1959, as he was beginning his not-quite-public campaign for the presidency, Lyndon Johnson traveled to Hyde Park to speak about his political hero, Franklin Roosevelt. Here is what Johnson said:

> He was a New Yorker and an Easterner. But one of the first tasks which he set himself was the raising up of the South, economic problem number one, still suffering from the destruction of capital in the War Between the States. He was an Easterner and a New Yorker, but the second important task he set himself was to bring to the West the electric power, the rural electrification and the water which it needed to grow. And the West and the South will forever love him— and follow where he led.

That love had begun to fade, of course, even before Johnson spoke, but his appreciation of Roosevelt's trans-regional empathy and economic and political smarts nonetheless rings true today. If they want to win more working-class votes, white and otherwise, and actually build the more equitable economy they seek, the Democrats could use some of that empathy, and lots of those smarts.

THE DEMOCRATS''WORKING CLASS PROBLEM'

It's not only with whites. It reaches well into the party's base.

Stanley B. Greenberg

The road to a sustainable Democratic majority—nationally, locally and in the states—must include much higher Democratic performance with white working class voters (those without a four-year degree). Nearly every group in the progressive infrastructure is busy figuring out how Democrats can get back to the level of support they reached with President Obama 2012 victory. That is a pretty modest target, however, given the scale of Democratic losses. It underestimates the scope of the problem and, ironically, the opportunity.

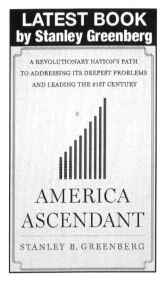

LATEST BOOK by Stanley Greenberg

A REVOLUTIONARY NATION'S PATH TO ADDRESSING ITS DEEPEST PROBLEMS AND LEADING THE 21ST CENTURY

AMERICA ASCENDANT

STANLEY B. GREENBERG

The Democrats don't have a 'white working class problem.' They have a 'working class problem,' that progressives have been reluctant to address honestly or boldly. The fact is Democrats have lost support with *all* working class voters across the electorate, including the Rising American Electorate of minorities, unmarried women and millennials. This decline contributed mightily to the Democrats' losses in the states and Congress and to the election of Donald Trump.

Also By Stan Greenberg:

Understanding the white working class Trump voter

In March 2017 Stan Greenberg conducted a profoundly important series of post-election focus groups with white working class Trump voters in Michigan. These discussions provide essential information for understanding the way these voters see the world and why they continue to support Trump and the GOP. The report systematically distinguishes both what they like about Trump and the areas where they disagree.

http://thedemocraticstrategist -roundtables.com/link

Stan Greenberg is the president of Greenberg, Quinlan, Rosner Research and Democracy Corps.

Fortunately, Democrats have the opportunity to consolidate, engage and perform much better with all of working America. I say "opportunity" advisedly, because better performance requires Democrats to embrace dramatically bolder economic policies and to attack a political economy that works for the rich, big corporations, and the cultural elites, but not for average Americans.

Bernie Sanders' "revolution" and attack on big money was much closer to hitting the mark than was Hillary Clinton's message, and he won millennials and white working class voters in the primary. It is not surprising that white working class voters then went for Trump, and that some Sanders voters went for the Green Party in the General Election, but the Democrats' working class problem go way beyond what Sanders broached.

What is the Democrats' working class problem?

Working class Americans pulled back from Democrats in this last period of Democratic governance because of President Obama's insistence on heralding economic progress and the bailout of the irresponsible elites, while ordinary people's incomes crashed and they continued to struggle financially. They also have pulled back because of the Democrats' seeming embrace of multi-national trade agreements that have cost American jobs. The Democrats have also moved from seeking to manage and champion the nation's growing immigrant diversity to seeming to champion immigrant rights over American citizens'. Not surprisingly and instinctively, the Democrats embraced the liberal values of America's dynamic and best-educated metropolitan areas, seeming not to respect the values or economic stress of older voters in small town and rural America. Finally, the Democrats also missed the economic stress and social problems in the cities themselves and working class suburbs.

These are big structural challenges, but we have plenty of evidence that they can be addressed and that Democrats can speak powerfully to these working class voters about them.

The core problem is President Obama's handling of the economy—and confronting this problem won't make me popular. The president and the Democrats heroically rescued America and the global economy, restored the soundness of the financial system and managed the economy back to a full recovery. But incomes for most Americans fell during this period and the top 1 percent took all of the income gains of the recovery—a subject that mainstream Democrats barely mentioned and did not fight to address. The president of the United States was the main messenger for the Democrats, and his consistent economic message to the country—from one year after the crash through last year's presidential election—was this: *the recession has been transformed into a dependable recovery, our economy is creating jobs and we are on the right track, but the Republicans drove our economy "into the ditch" and are doing everything possible to obstruct our progress.* He closed the 2016 election with this appeal: *we created 15.5 million new jobs, incomes are rising, poverty is falling, and you must get out and vote to "build on our progress."*

Closely bound up with the "progress" narrative was the bailout of the Wall Street banks with taxpayer money. Wall Street excess took the country's economy off a cliff and Democrats rightly came to the nation's rescue by passing TARP. But the bailout of the banks was, and remains, a searing event in American consciousness—and one inextricably linked to Democratic governance. While the bailout came at the urging of President Bush and his treasury secretary, it was embraced by then candidate Obama and passed with Democratic votes in the House and Senate. It was under President Obama that the government signed off on the executive bonuses for TARP recipients and under Obama that no executive was punished for criminal malfeasance. It should come as no surprise, then, that one year after the Economic Recovery Act's passage, the majority of voters thought the big banks, not the middle class, were the main beneficiaries—and they were damn angry about it too.

That mix of heralding "progress" while bailing out those responsible for the crisis and the real crash in incomes for working Americans was a fatal brew for Democrats. It was evident in the double-digit drop in Obama's approval ratings in Maine, Michigan, Minnesota, New Hampshire, and Pennsylvania in 2010. (Note this is 2010, not 2016.) His approval rating rebounded to nearly 50 percent in most of those states in 2012, but it fell sharply in 2014 in Florida, and North Carolina, New Hampshire and Maine, Wisconsin, Ohio, Michigan and Minnesota. Obama's approval rating in the year before the 2016 election hovered between 40 and 42 percent in Iowa, Maine, New Hampshire, and Ohio.

Obama Approval in Key States

	2009	2010	2011	2012	2013	2014	2015
Florida	57%	46%	43%	48%	47%	42%	46%
Iowa	57%	47%	46%	49%	42%	37%	41%
Maine	59%	47%	47%	50%	45%	45%	41%
Michigan	60%	49%	48%	51%	48%	43%	47%
Minnesota	61%	48%	48%	50%	48%	45%	47%
New Hampshire	55%	41%	39%	46%	44%	39%	40%
North Carolina	55%	47%	44%	47%	43%	41%	44%
Ohio	55%	47%	42%	47%	42%	39%	42%
Pennsylvania	57%	46%	45%	47%	43%	42%	43%
Wisconsin	58%	48%	47%	50%	46%	42%	45%

Source: Gallup

These are the states that figured in the well-told retreat of white working class voters from the Democrats. But introspection among progressives—including those at the White House—failed to see the retreat of hard-pressed working class voters in the new American majority of minorities, unmarried women and millennials, most of whom do not have a four-year degree. While the president was calling on these base voters to come to the polls to defend the progress we'd presumably made, these voters, too, were angry about the claims about jobs and about Wall Street's undimmed influence. They knew these jobs paid dramatically less. They saw the government rescue the big banks but do next to nothing about the home foreclosures and lost wealth in their Hispanic and black communities. That is why about 40 percent of the Rising American Electorate disapproved of how the president was doing his job in both 2010 and 2014. Every segment of this progressive base underperformed on vote and turnout in 2010, and their disengagement in 2014 gave us the lowest off-year turnout in any election since World War II and with it, another Republican-wave.

The electoral consequences were particularly acute among millennials. Weighed down by student debt and the weak job market, millennials pulled back in 2010 and importantly, did not come back in 2012 when Barack Obama was on the ballot. Their vote share was down 2 points from 2008 (from 17 to 15 percent), and their level of support for Obama was down 9 points (from 69 to 60 percent). Mitt Romney won the white millennials by 7 points.

Democrats' unified control of government under President Obama and the Democratic Congress began losing working class Americans' support right from the outset, but progressives collectively never paused to take stock of why.

Trade is the next issue that has separated Democrats from many working class voters. That separation grew wider with President Obama's battle for the Trans-Pacific Partnership and with Donald Trump making his opposition to it central to his vow to represent "the forgotten Americans."

In 2015, fully 72 percent of Democrats in the Senate (33 of 46) and 85 percent of Democrats in the House (160 of 188) had voted against giving President Obama fast-track authority to negotiate the TPP. The party's presidential candidates were strongly opposed to corporate lobbyists dominating the drafting of TPP and to major provisions that would have granted foreign corporations the right to sue for damages over U.S. consumer and environmental protections. But working class Americans clearly associate Democrats with support for multi-national trade agreements—even though they are passed with mostly Republican votes in the Congress—because Democratic presidents have been their main champions over the last twenty-five years. NAFTA was enacted under President Clinton (with my support as I was then the president's pollster and over the very strong objections of my wife, Rep. Rosa DeLauro). President Obama made passage of TPP a consuming priority at the end of his presidency.

Support for trade and trade agreements is greatest on the West and East coasts, among Hispanics and Asians, and most importantly, among college graduates, particularly in the big cities where Democrats govern. But the white working class, who live amidst the remains of the manufacturing sector in the industrial Midwest, strongly oppose these trade agreements with increasing ferocity, particularly the men who were disproportionately employed in manufacturing.

Class and gender and TPP

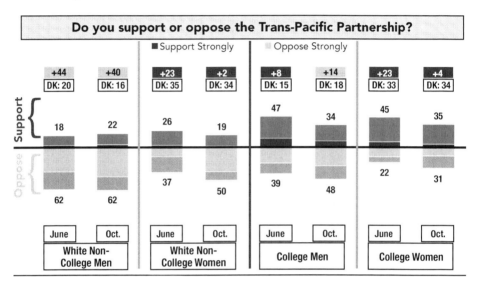

Source: Democracy Corps survey of national likely voters for Public Citizen, October 2016.

The Obama presidency produced a partisan re-alignment on trade, re-enforcing the class and gender bases of the two parties that will disrupt the politics of both, if it hasn't already. Before 2008, Republicans were more supportive of NAFTA than Democrats, but at the end of Obama's presidency, GOP support for NAFTA collapsed, pushed off the cliff by Trump. Democrats, on the other hand, became more favorably disposed to NAFTA.

Partisans Flip on NAFTA:

Biggest drop in GOP support for NAFTA in decade over 6 months

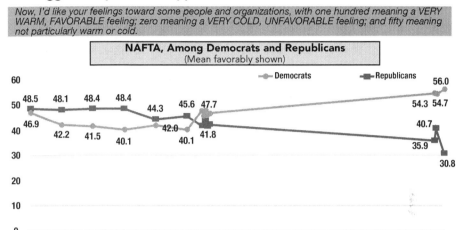

Source: Democracy Corps survey of national likely voters for Public Citizen, October 2016.

With Trump centering his campaign on bringing back American jobs by withdrawing from and renegotiating trade agreements, the Republican base votes emerged as those most opposed to multi-national trade agreements.

Despite Obama's efforts, Democratic voters also shifted against trade in principle and the TPP specifically over the course of the campaign—including big shifts among millennials (a 22 point shift in margin), white unmarried women (21 point margin shift), all unmarried women (15 points) and minority voters (9 points). Yet Hillary Clinton went silent on TPP in the closing weeks of her campaign, even as Obama and his administration stumped publicly for its enactment, though there was virtually no chance a lame duck Congress would pass it. That magnified the Democrats' working America problem and perhaps decisively so in the Rust Belt.

Immigration is the next critical element of the Democrats' working class challenge. Since 1990, the world has watched a massive increase in global migration, and, remarkably, one in five of these migrants live in the United States. The number of immigrants in the United States doubled from 20 million to 46 million during this time and our largest metropolitan areas are being shaped by accelerating migration and the numbers of foreign-born living there. More than three million, roughly 37 percent, of New York City residents were born outside of the United States; 60 percent of Miami's residents and almost 30 percent of Houston's residents are foreign-born.[1]

Despite Donald Trump's ascendance, America remains one of the few places in the world that views immigration as positive, but Americans' reactions have a strong class and race component that re-enforce the conclusion that there is a working class challenge that cuts across partisan lines. In Democracy Corps' election night survey, it was white college educated women who embraced immigration most strongly, and not surprisingly, white working class men who were most cautious. But do not assume that African Americans do not share some of those concerns; many in our focus groups raise anxieties about competition from new immigrants.

% AGREE BY WHITE GENDER EDUCATION	Immigrants today strengthen our country because of their hard work and talents.	Immigrants today are a burden on our country because they take our jobs, housing and health
White non-college men	42% agree	45% agree
White non-college women	40% agree	40% agree
White college men	58% agree	29% agree
White college women	68% agree	22% agree

Source: Democracy Corps Election Night survey of 2016 voters for WVWVAF & Roosevelt Institute.

But reactions to legalization of the undocumented reveal some of the emotional and economic dynamics at play. Americans are fairly positive about the economic effects of legalization and see many of these immigrants as hard working, but they do worry about the costs. Over 60 percent believe granting legal status would lead to greater competition for public services and over half believe it would take jobs from American

---

[1]See "5 facts about the U.S. rank in worldwide migration," Pew Research Center, May 18, 2016; See U.S. Census.

citizens. Those numbers are not driven entirely by Republicans. Indeed, 41 percent of Democrats think the legalized would "take jobs from U.S. citizens" and more important, half of Democrats believe granting legal status "would be a drain on government services."

Perceived costs of legalization:

Most Republicans See Economic Benefits from Legalization, But Worry about Costs

% who agree with statements about undocumented immigrants in U.S.	Total %	Rep %	Dem %	Ind %	Diff
Deporting all undocumented immigrants is unrealistic	77	76	80	78	D+4
Better for the economy if they become legal workers	75	70	83	74	D+13
Most are hard workers who should have opportunity to improve their lives	75	69	81	73	D+12
Granting legal status would encourage more to come illegally	64	77	53	68	R+24
Granting legal status would be a drain on government services	61	72	50	63	R+22
Granting legal services would reward illegal behaviour	54	68	41	56	R+27
Granting legal status would take jobs from U.S. citizens	51	66	41	51	R+25

PEW RESEARCH CENTER/USA TODAY June 12-16, 2013, Q55 a-g.

Source: Pew Research Center/ USA Today national survey, June 12-16, 2013.

President Obama, who led the battle for immigration reform, was fairly trusted on this issue as he always began by defining "real reform." It means "stronger border security" and his administration did in fact put "more boots on the Southern border than at any time in our history." "Real reform" also meant "establishing a responsible pathway to earned citizenship" that included "paying taxes and a meaningful penalty" and "going to the back of the line behind the folks trying to come here legally."[2]

Pro-immigration advocates won majority support for comprehensive immigration reform only after the public became confident that leaders wanted to manage immigration and that they took borders and citizenship seriously. The reform that passed the U.S. Senate increased enforcement

---

[2]President Obama's 2013 State of the Union Address.

at the border, introduced new technology to ensure lawful employment, expelled those with criminal records and allowed a path to citizenship for those who paid a fine and back taxes and learned English. That combination allowed progressives to proudly advocate a new law that would greatly expand the number of legal immigrants and make America more culturally and economically dynamic.

By the time Hillary Clinton was running in 2016, however, the path to citizenship moved to the center of her offer, as well as concern for immigrant rights in the face of Trump's promised Muslim ban and Mexican border wall.

A month into Trump's presidency Democracy Corps and the Roosevelt Institute conducted focus groups with white working class Trump voters who had previously supported Obama in Macomb County, Michigan. It was clear how central concerns about immigration, borders, foreignness and Islam were to their receptivity to his call to take back America. Many thought Hillary Clinton, on the other hand, wanted "open borders."

I am confident Democrats will once again lead a multicultural America in the same way America has forged unity from such diversity in the past. We build on a unique framework for immigration and a unique history. Even this ugly interlude will not keep America from its exceptional path.

The final dynamic distancing Democrats from working class America is their alignment with the economically and culturally ascendant in America's metropolitan centers where Democrats win office and govern. As Clinton's winning popular vote margin grew to 3 million, concentrated in an ever smaller number of urban counties, The Brookings Institute revealed that fewer than 500 Clinton-won counties produced two-thirds of the nation's GDP in 2015.

Perhaps that is why President Obama and Secretary Clinton sounded so satisfied with the state of America and its future. In nearly every speech for most of his presidency, including in his 2014 State of the Union Address, President Obama rightly declared America "is better-positioned for the twenty-first century than any other nation on Earth." When he and Hillary Clinton closed the 2016 campaign in Philadelphia, Detroit,

Miami, Chicago, Raleigh, Cleveland and Columbus with their upbeat take on America's future, they symbolically aligned the Democrats nationally with the economically ascendant cities—and they barely noticed anything amiss in smaller cities and towns and rural America.

They were also aligning the national Democrats with a liberal narrative and moral frame that values equality, equal rights and fairness. They are more empathetic and worry more about harm to the vulnerable. They are more open to diversity and celebrate differences and outside cultures. They value a kind of individualism that emphasizes personal autonomy, self-expression, and sexual freedom for men and women. They welcome the emerging pluralism of family types and reject the traditional family and gender roles. Education is the path to individual fulfillment and opportunity, and science and technology are the keys to learning discoverable truths. They consciously do not turn to traditional authority for moral absolutes, and they devalue those who depend on faith-based conclusions.

Those who hold to a conservative moral frame, by contrast, accept faith-based moral absolutes and respect traditional authority. They honor an individualism that is grounded in personal responsibility, industriousness, strong work ethic, self-reliance, self-restraint, and self-discipline that guard against idleness and dependence. They honor the traditional family and the male breadwinner role. They value patriotism, love of country, and those who defend it from our enemies and believe American citizens come first.

What the national Democrats' embrace of the liberal moral frame and America's economic ascendance misses is not just the plight of non-metropolitan America, but also the reality on the ground in the big cities, which are ground zero for our country's greatest challenges. Any Democrat running for mayor in New York, Chicago or Los Angeles knows that, which is why Mayor Bill de Blasio's critique of "Two New Yorks" was so resonant. It is there where large numbers of residents are struggling economically with low wage jobs and the sky-high cost of living, where poverty and segregation stubbornly persist, where millions of children are raised by single parents, and where inequality is most stark. At the same time, the increasingly diverse ethnic and racial mix in the cities is full of working class communities where both liberal and conservative moral frames matter. For example, like the more conservative working class whites, African American women place a high premium on faith in God and the need to put American citizens before immigrants. That is why the simple embrace of metropolitan America's liberal values and economic elite hurt Democrats with working class voters in both the big cities and rural America.

Fixing the Democrats' working class problem

The rift between Democrats and working class Americans was painfully widened by how Democrats governed and campaigned nationally. The party was not up to the great challenge of leading an America that is more culturally diverse and racially conflicted, more urban and younger, more economically and socially unequal and more corrupt. All of those challenges, however, are also a call to action.

After the 2014 debacle and in advance of the 2016 presidential cycle, the Women's Voices Women's Vote Action Fund, with which Democracy Corps partners, produced a frank report on disappointing results in our base. They highlighted the unmarried women whose vote for Democrats dropped 7 points from 2012, and the fact that Democrats lost white unmarried women by 2 points. That is when we made the connection between white unmarried women and the white working class women who are now a majority of the white working class.

Both groups see only a precarious path to the middle class. Both believe jobs don't pay enough to live on and that the middle class pays a lot of taxes. Both groups, more than other voters in the Rising American Electorate, expressed concern about welfare spending and getting control of the borders. When we tested a bold Democratic economic agenda against the Republican agenda, white unmarried women embraced the Democratic offer with great enthusiasm, and this agenda trailed the Republican offer by only 8 points among white working class women. The results were so promising we proposed at the outset of the 2016 cycle that progressives adopt an "RAE+" strategy to reach the working class more broadly.

Given how disastrously Clinton performed with white working class voters in the end, it is important to recall with data that she was poised to *over-perform* with the white working class women compared to Obama in

2012. Mitt Romney won white working class women by 17 points. During the presidential debates, Clinton closed Trump's margin with white working class women to just 4 points in NBC/WSJ's national polling—and those voters did not break away from her until the last week, after Clinton went silent on the economy and change. These white working class women, who form a majority of today's white working class, were open to voting for Clinton, perhaps in historic numbers.

White working class 2016 president vote

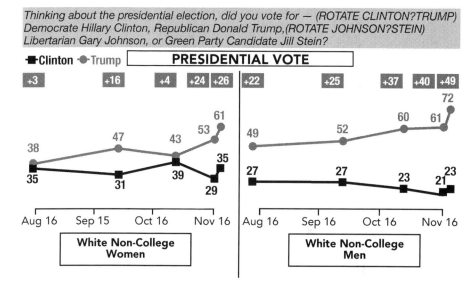

Source: NBC/WSJ national likely vote surveys, 2016.

Not surprisingly, white working class women form a big portion (40 percent) of the independents and Democrats who voted for Trump in the end. While Republican Trump voters think of themselves as middle class, and two-thirds say they would have no problem handling an unexpected $500 expense, these non-GOP Trump voters think of themselves as working class and would struggle to handle the sudden expense. They are also, in contrast to the Trump Republicans, pro-union.

But, in what may border on campaign malpractice, the Clinton campaign chose in the closing battle to ignore the economic stress not just of the working class women who were still in play, but also of those within the

Democrats' own base, particularly among the minorities, millennials, and unmarried women. It likely diminished turnout in the cities and Clinton's vote across the base.

President Obama's final campaign speeches spoke of an economy that moved from recession to recovery and created 15.5 million jobs with rising incomes and reduced poverty. But if you look at people's view of the economy on the night of the election, three-in-five scorned that rosy economic outlook—led by nearly every group in the Democrats' base. "Jobs don't pay enough to live on and it is a struggle to save anything," said 70 percent of minorities and 65 percent of unmarried women in our post-election survey. A majority of unmarried women said they could not handle an unexpected $500 expense, putting them most on the edge. That is the heart of the Rising American Electorate and their judgment on the economy was very close to white working class women's.

Everyone agrees it is a struggle to get by today

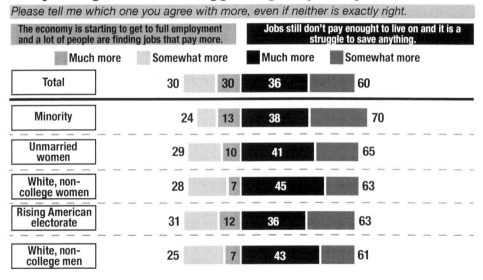

Please tell me which one you agree with more, even if neither is exactly right.

	The economy is starting to get to full employment and a lot of people are finding jobs that pay more.		Jobs still don't pay enought to live on and it is a struggle to save anything.	
	Much more	Somewhat more	Much more	Somewhat more
Total	30	30	36	60
Minority	24	13	38	70
Unmarried women	29	10	41	65
White, non-college women	28	7	45	63
Rising American electorate	31	12	36	63
White, non-college men	25	7	43	61

Source: Democracy Corps Election Night survey of 2016 voters for the Roosevelt Institute.

The failure to see that the problems of working America run right through the new American majority cost the campaign a chance to produce a very different result in this election.

As I have written in *The Guardian* and *Democracy Journal*, Clinton's strong performance in the debates produced big gains for her on which candidate is better suited to handle the economy and taxes, stand up for the middle class and against special interests. After the debates, she was near parity with Trump on handling the economy—closing an 11-point pre-convention gap.

Democracy Corps' national survey conducted after the debates and shared with the Clinton campaign showed that more attacks on Trump's temperament, treatment of people and women barely moved voters. By contrast, a compelling economic message demanding "an economy for everyone, not just the rich and well connected," attacking "trickle down" tax cuts "for the richest and special breaks for corporations," and promising an agenda to "rebuild the middle class" moved unmarried women, including white unmarried women, millennials and white working class women.

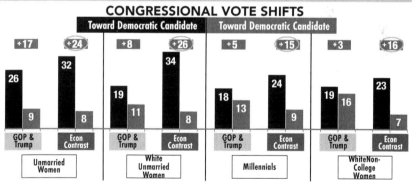

Source: Democracy Corps national likely voter survey, October 2016.

The failure to see that the problems of working America run right through This experiment showed—retrospectively, alas—that Democrats can reach working class Americans both in our base and well into the swing electorate, including the white working class. It is time to make that challenge task number one.

DEMOCRATS NEED TO BE THE PARTY OF AND FOR WORKING PEOPLE—OF ALL RACES.

Robert Griffin, John Halpin and Ruy Teixeira

Since November, progressives have engaged in many solid post-election audits seeking to explain how the Obama coalition was narrowly supplanted by Donald Trump's ethno-nationalist wave of white working class support. Analysts have explored the relative balance of economic versus racial factors; the breakdown in polling, field organizing, and message development; and the role of campaign-specific mistakes and external interventions by the FBI, WikiLeaks, and the Russians. In an election decided by small margins in a handful of states, each of these factors arguably played a role.

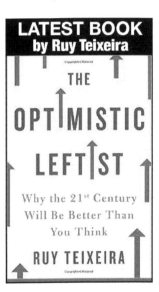

LATEST BOOK by Ruy Teixeira

THE OPTIMISTIC LEFTIST

Why the 21ˢᵗ Century Will Be Better Than You Think

RUY TEIXEIRA

New York Magazine Interview with Ruy Teixeira
In a March 2017 interview, Ruy Teixeira discussed the importance of the white working class for Democrats and why the rise of the "Obama coalition" did not eliminate the need to maintain significant support among this group. Teixeira outlines the way in which the argument of The Emerging Democratic Majority became reduced to the notion of "demographic inevitability."

http://nymag.com/daily/intelligencer/2017/03/can-the-democrats-still-count-on-a-demographic-advantage.html

Robert Griffin, John Halpin and Ruy Teixeira are senior fellows at the Center for American Progress.

Unfortunately, this process has led to some unfruitful debates about whether progressives should double down on the Obama coalition voters, reach out more to white working class voters, or appeal more to independent and conservative-leaning suburban whites.

ROBERT GRIFFIN, JOHN HALPIN AND RUY TEIXEIRA

When a party narrowly loses the Electoral College it successfully won in two consecutive presidential cycles, and is down hundreds of seats at the state and local level, however, it does not have the luxury of fine tuning which voters it will reach out to over the next few years.

Democrats need to reach out to all types of voters across a large swath of the country.

The idea that the Democrats should or could afford to ignore white working class voters, particularly at the state and local level, defies basic political math. Although we've written extensively about how the nation's shifting demographics and ideological attitudes helped to fuel the rise of the Obama coalition, none of these trends preclude the need to build cross-racial and cross-class coalitions in more places.

More diverse, younger, socially liberal, and Democratic-leaning voters are not evenly distributed across the nation, and even with the long-term expected declines in white working class populations, these voters alone cannot sustain successful Democratic coalitions going forward. Democrats do not need to win FDR-level support among white working class voters, but they cannot afford to lose them by margins as high as 30 to 40 points in some key states—as they have in recent elections.

White Working Class Trends

In 1980, the white working class (WWC) composed about 70 percent of the eligible voter population. As a result of the changing racial composition of the country and the rising rates of educational attainment, the next 36 years saw this group decline by 25 points—down to 45 percent of all eligible voters. While the WWC is still the largest race/education group in the country, it ceased to be the majority of eligible voters around 2010.

Neither the 1980 geographic distribution of this population nor the changes since have been homogenous, however. As you can see in Figure 1, even in 1980 the white working class population was more concentrated in the nation's interior as well as the Pacific Northwest and deep Northeast. At the time, only two states had an eligible population that was less than 50 percent WWC—New Mexico and Hawaii.

Figure 1—White Working Class as Percentage of Eligible Voters

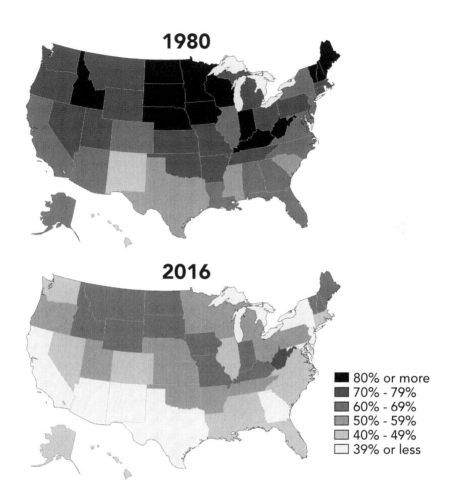

Fast forwarding to 2016, the 25 percentage point national decline of white working class voters as a percentage of eligible voters had an impact just about everywhere. However, the change was especially concentrated along the coasts of the country and in those states with economically attractive metropolitan areas, drawing both newer immigrants and college-educated whites.

Using a more detailed geographical breakdown, Figure 2 displays the percent of the voting age population that is WWC in each county in the United States. Going deeper than the state level, we can see that the highest concentration counties are clustered in Appalachia, extending northeast (but shying away from the coast) and northwest through the Midwest, Great Lake region, and the Dakotas.

Figure 2—White Working Class as Percentage of Voting Age Population

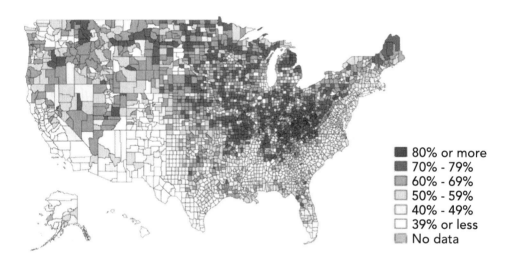

80% or more
70% - 79%
60% - 69%
50% - 59%
40% - 49%
39% or less
No data

To see a color version of this map go to: [http://thedemocraticstrate-gist-roundtables.com/democrats-need-to-be-the-party-of-and-for-work-ing-people-of-all-races/]

Although educational projections are difficult, our own calculations suggest that we'll see declines in the WWC population continue well into the future. Even if we assume that college attainment rates flatten out rather than grow (an assumption that runs counter to current trends), the continuing racial diversification of the nation will cause this group to shrink. We anticipate that the WWC will constitute just 43 percent of eligible voters by 2020, 35 percent by 2040, and 28 percent by 2060.

Despite the demographic decline that has already occurred for this group and the similarly sized decline likely to come over the next 44 years, the white working class maintains a large political presence in America. Why?

Although a variety of explanations could be proffered, one of the simplest and most compelling is this: The WWC is very well distributed geographically for the purposes of political influence. They are disproportionately concentrated in swing[1] states, as the maps above suggest. But they are also disproportionately concentrated in swing congressional districts. And they are especially concentrated in swing congressional districts within swing states. In Rust Belt states, for example, the typical swing district was 11 points more WWC than the average district across the nation, and 16 points less minority. In short, they live where it counts.

How did these trends affect the 2016 election? We can say a few things with a high amount of certainty.

Whites—including those without college degrees—turned out at a higher rate than they did in 2012. Turnout in the nation as whole was up—probably to the tune of about 1.6 points.[2] Two pieces of data point to rising white turnout as the cause—particularly among WWC eligible voters.

First, data recently released in November supplement of the Current Population Survey—commonly regarded as the gold standard for estimating turnout among specific demographic groups—indicate that White turnout was up overall compared to 2012. Looking at Table 1, we can see that this increase in participation was concentrated among non-college whites.

[1] Defined here as congressional districts scoring between +5R and +5D on The Cook Partisan Voting Index.
[2] Based on estimates from the United States Elections Project. Data available at http://www.electproject.org/home/voter-turnout/voter-turnout-data.

Table 1: Turnout Rates in the 2012 and 2016 Presidential Elections Among Eligible Voters

	2012 Turnout	2016 Turnout	Difference[3]
White, Non-College	57.0	57.8	+0.7
White, College	79.0	79.1	+0.2
Black	66.6	59.6	-7.1
Hispanic	48.0	47.6	-0.4
Asian	47.1	48.8	+1.7
Other	55.3	50.4	-4.9

There is also evidence of rising WWC turnout from election data we have at the county level. Looking at Figure 3, we can see there is a positive relationship between the percent of a county that is WWC and the change in turnout between 2016 and 2012. That is, the counties where the voting-age population was largely WWC are also places that saw increases in their turnout, a pattern that suggests WWC turnout was also up this election cycle.

[3] Difference may not match displayed numbers due to rounding.

Figure 3—Change in Turnout by WWC Percentage in County

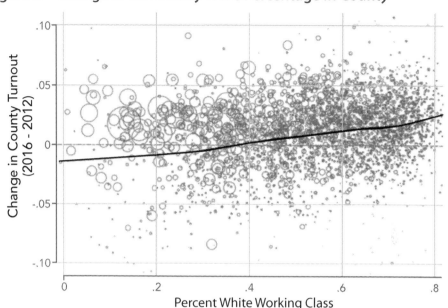

Clinton made gains among white, college educated voters while Trump gained among white, non-college voters. Multiple sources of data and accounts confirm that, compared with Romney, Trump improved his margins within the WWC while losing ground with white, college-educated voters. According to the National Election Pool exit polls, these figures were just about a positive 14-point shift and negative 10-point shift, respectively. Assuming those national figures are true, how much of the county-by-county shift in the vote can be accounted for by combining information about the percentage of the voting-age population that is college and non-college white in a given county with the national-level margin shifts? Put another way, if we assumed that all white college and non-college voters everywhere shifted by the amount that was recorded in the national exit polls, how well would that line up with the actual change in vote shares we saw on Election Day? As seen in Figure 4, there is a very strong relationship between this simulated shift and the margin shift we actually saw at the county level.

Figure 4—Estimated Shift vs. Actual Shift

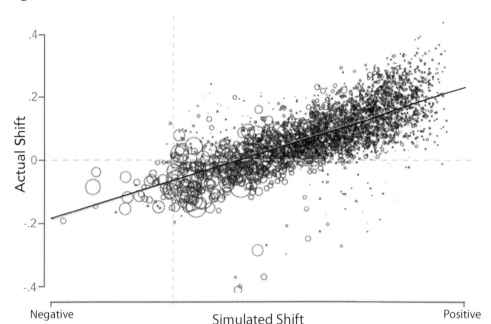

Beyond confirming that these data points from the exit polls seem consistent with the actual results we saw on Election Day, this exercise is also useful because it allows us to see where the model fails. That is, while we see a strong, linear relationship between our simulated shift and the actual shift observed on Election Day, it is not a perfect relationship—the data points in Figure 4 fall both above and below the blue line. The question is, are there geographic regions where this simulated shift systematically overestimates or underestimates the actual shift? That is, are there areas where we saw a smaller or larger shift to Trump than we would expect given that national margin shift among the WWC and college whites?

Looking at Figure 5, which displays the residuals from the model displayed in Figure 5, we can see that there are strong regional patterns. The areas in red are places where our model underestimated the shift (that is, Trump did better than we would expect given both the national shift among WWC and college whites and the proportions of these two groups in the county), while the areas in blue overestimated the shift (that is, Trump did worse than we would expect).

As can be seen, there is a significant under-estimation of Trump's gains relative to Romney in the Northeast, Midwest, Great Lakes region, and the Dakotas. The relatively low levels of non-whites in most of these counties, particularly as you get away from the coastal areas in the Northeast, means it is less likely that a change in these populations' behaviors (turnout or vote choice) could account for this under-estimation. This implies that Trump in these areas either a) had larger shifts in his direction among whites, probably due to relatively large margin shifts among white noncollege voters, or b) benefitted from higher relative turnout from WWC populations, or c) some combination of both.

Figure 5—Model Residuals of Trump Support

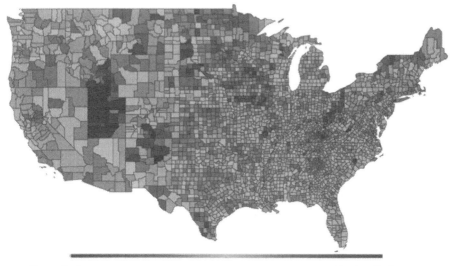

Over-Estimate   Under-Estimate

To see a color version of this map go to: [http://thedemocraticstrate-gist-roundtables.com/democrats-need-to-be-the-party-of-and-for-work-ing-people-of-all-races/]

In contrast, the South was generally a region where we saw smaller actual margin shifts than we would have expected given the data from the exit polls. There are a variety of ways to make sense of that data, but the most straightforward explanation is probably the correct one: This was a region of the country where whites were already conservative enough that they couldn't realistically shift their vote margins further rightward to the degree we observed at the national levels.

The Southwest, California, and Texas are home to some of the most Hispanic counties in the country. Where we see strong blue patterning, this could suggest a bit of a counterpunch by Hispanics, with potentially higher Hispanic turnout and vote margins offsetting the expected gains we thought we would see given the vote-choice shift among whites. Additionally, we might be seeing something similar to the South—a white population that is already so conservative (though not in coastal California) that it didn't change as much as whites nationwide.

That said, there is also a strong red streak of underestimation coming up from the southern tip of Texas, hugging the border westward, and extending up into New Mexico. Puzzlingly, we can see in Figure 7 that these are actually some of the most heavily Hispanic counties in the nation.

How do we make sense of this given the relationships we discussed in the previous paragraphs? Interestingly, the same rural-urban divide that we've long recognized as an important cleavage in the white population might have played a role here. Specifically, while Trump likely did poorly among Hispanics as a whole, it's possible that his margins were somewhat better among this group's rural populations, a finding supported by analysis of precinct data in Texas. Those highly Hispanic counties that we also identified as having smaller shifts than we'd expect generally have relatively low population density.

Figure 6—Percent Hispanic by County

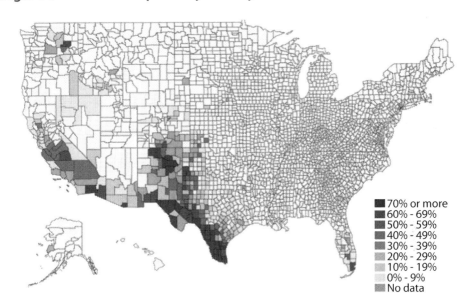

To see a color version of this map go to: [http://thedemocraticstrate-gist-roundtables.com/democrats-need-to-be-the-party-of-and-for-working-people-of-all-races/]

As we head into the Pacific Northwest we notice a strong blue pattern of over-estimation in Washington and Oregon despite large white populations. This is in stark contrast to its counterparts in the white and rural counties of the Northeast. It's possible that college and non-college whites in this notably progressive region of the country shifted, respectively, further away and not as hard toward Trump. Additionally, as we can see in Figure 8, this was also a region of the country where a significant portion of the vote went toward third-party candidates. To the extent that Clinton lost ground compared with Obama in 2012, it would appear to be the case that many voters shifted toward Gary Johnson and Jill Stein.

Lastly, Utah is undoubtedly the political outlier of the 2016 election. During the Republican primary, Trump was denounced by Mitt Romney and faced a conservative and Mormon independent candidate, Evan

McMullin, who captured an impressive 21.3 percent of the vote. Trump underperformed spectacularly in this state and, as a result, our simple model overestimates the gains he should have made given the demographic composition of the state.

Figure 7—Third Party Vote by County

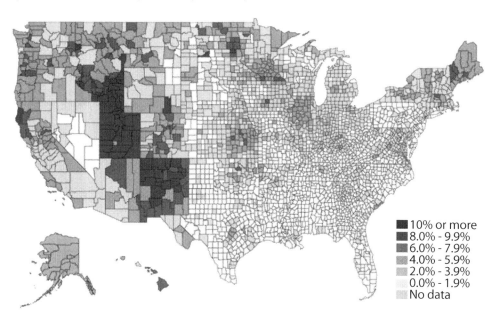

To see a color version of this map go to: [http://thedemocraticstrategist-roundtables.com/democrats-need-to-be-the-party-of-and-for-working-people-of-all-races/]

Strategy Going Forward

What do these preliminary findings tell us about Democratic Party strategy and coalition-building in the Trump era?

For starters, rather than debating whether Democrats should appeal to white working-class voters or voters of color—both necessary components of a successful electoral coalition, particularly at the state and local level—a more important question emerges: Why are Democrats losing support and seeing declining turnout from working-class voters of all races in many places?

This is just a hypothesis, but in an era of widespread political cynicism, economic and cultural anxiety, and distrust of both business and government, the Democrats allowed themselves to become the party of the status quo—a status quo perceived to be elitist, exclusionary, and disconnected from the entire range of working-class concerns, but particularly from those voters in white working-class areas. Rightly or wrongly, Hillary Clinton's campaign exemplified a professional-class status quo that failed to rally enough working-class voters of color and failed to blunt the drift of white working-class voters to Republicans.

The Democrats' strength on social and cultural issues helped them build a national popular-vote majority with high levels of support in deep-blue cities and states. But after eight years of Obama, Democrats were simply unable to make a credible case to working-class voters of all races, in the states and regions that mattered most, that they could deliver on working-class voters' core economic needs or represent their values and concerns.

Donald Trump played this card perfectly, first taking over his own sclerotic party and then successfully stitching together a targeted Electoral College victory by promising serious change and embodying a completely different approach to politics than either traditional Democrats or Republicans could offer.

Examining the Center for American Progress's post-election survey, a full 50 percent of Trump voters said the most important influence on their vote in 2016 was that they wanted "to vote for Trump and the chance to shake up the political establishment," compared with 29 percent who voted mainly for the policy agenda of the Republicans and another 21 percent who said they voted mainly against Clinton. A similar percentage of Trump voters (50 percent) said they strongly agreed with the idea that "Ordinary people's opinions are more honest and correct than those of experts in politics and the media," compared with only 29 percent of Clinton voters. Although it's likely these attitudes did not dominate other racial or economic considerations that drove people to Trump, the overall conditions for populist voting were clear throughout the entire primary and general election cycles. Democrats can chew over tactical improvements to their campaigns and outreach, but in the absence of a broad party unifier like Obama, they desperately need to reexamine the public face, leadership, agenda, and ideological approach of the party, given this larger populist context. Voters are in no mood for traditional politics carried out by people they feel are out of touch with their everyday needs and values.

The party needs to rediscover its roots as a working-class party, one that was initially exclusionary of people of color but that today can and must represent the interests and values of working people of all races. As the party fights Trump and his brand of divisive right-wing populism, the party needs to bring in more working-class candidates and leaders who can credibly talk with their communities about common economic and social challenges, can forcefully take on the corporate interests that harm these communities, and who can be trusted to fight for the well-being and security of all working men and women.

If not, the Democrats risk ceding the mantle of political change, and possibly losing more elections, to a demagogic billionaire who talks about populist disruption while doing little to help workers and their families, and much to aid his wealthy cohorts.

BRIDGING THE DIVIDE
Helping to Rebuild a Multiracial Progressive Coalition by Winning Back White Working-Class Moderates

Matt Morrison

I. DEEP AND WIDE: Understanding the Full Magnitude of the Democrats' Defeat

Even before the election, political analysts were decrying Hillary Clinton as a candidate. She wasn't a natural campaigner. She wasn't spending enough time on the ground. She had too much baggage. She couldn't break through the noise about her email server. The natural extension of this argument is that a typical Democrat would have performed better than Clinton did and will in the future. However, the election results in key battleground states do not support this theory. Democrats lost up and down the ballot. And they have been losing cycle after cycle in non-urban America for some time.

By the middle of the 2016 cycle, there were nine competitive Senate races around the country: Florida, Indiana, Missouri, Nevada, New Hampshire, North Carolina,

What is Working America?

With over three million members, Working America, the community affiliate of the AFL-CIO, is the largest progressive organization that conducts door to door community organizing, focusing particularly on white working class communities. In 2016 Working America's field canvassers conducted an extraordinary one million front porch conversations and signed up 184,000 new members. As part of its organizing, Working America systematically collects uniquely valuable data on attitudes and strategies of persuasion.

Matt Morrison is the Political Director of Working America

Ohio, Pennsylvania and Wisconsin. Heading into 2016, Democrats felt confident about this favorable map, but Republicans ended up winning seven of those contests. In New Hampshire, Democrats staggered to a narrow 1,017-vote (0.14%) victory, and only in Nevada did the party record a healthy win. Notably, in both of these two states, Clinton had a clearer ground game advantage over Trump than in the places Democrats lost.

Democrats Fall Even Further Behind in the States

Democrats also came up short in state legislative races around the country. Of the 7,383 state legislators in America, Republicans grew their margin by 90 seats in 2016. Building off of big Democratic losses in 2014 at the state level, Republicans currently occupy 1,038 more state legislative seats than Democrats nationwide. They now control 68 of 99 legislative chambers and 32 of 50 governorships.

We believe that these massive losses up and down the ballot indicate problems that are much bigger than any weakness Clinton might have had as a candidate or any drag she might have had on the rest of the ticket.

Democrats have been losing small-town, exurban and rural voters cycle after cycle when Obama is not on the ballot. The consistency of those losses is illustrated in recent election results from our five states.

In the 2014 Michigan gubernatorial race, unsuccessful Democrat Mark Schauer received 43.09 percent of the vote in the non-urban counties. Clinton's 2016 performance fell a bit further behind his result (38.26%). In contrast, Obama received 49.28 percent of the vote in these same counties in 2012. Both Schauer and Clinton lost the state, yet Obama won it twice.

- In the 2010 and 2014 Wisconsin gubernatorial races, unsuccessful Democrats Tom Barrett and Mary Burke received 41.61 percent and 41.27 percent, respectively, in non-urban counties. Clinton's 2016 performance tracks slightly behind these benchmarks (39.38%) and was 7.5 points behind Obama (46.77%). This difference was a large part of the reason that Obama won Wisconsin twice while other Democrats lost.

- This same pattern held true in the North Carolina, Ohio and Pennsylvania midterm elections. Since 2008, Democrats have resoundingly lost the elections where Obama was not on the ballot, with a substantial share of those losses coming from a lack of support from working-class voters, especially in non-urban areas.

II. LOSING GROUND: The Loss of White Working-Class Swing Voters and Its Impact on Democrats

Much post-election analysis has focused on the drop in turnout among African-American voters. While we think lower turnout in this bedrock of the progressive base was a factor in some places, African-American turnout was not down everywhere. It did dip in crucial cities like Detroit and Cleveland, but turnout was up in other heavily African-American communities like Greensboro. Where there was a drop in turnout, it was not decisive for most states and in no state was it the largest share of vote loss.

Analyzing the Impact of African-American Turnout on Battleground State Losses

Some election postmortems hold that if we can just return African-American turnout to 2008 or 2012 levels, then Democrats will win again. Putting aside the importance of having a historic African-American presidential candidate the caliber of Barack Obama to reach 2008 and 2012 African-American turnout levels, high African-American turnout in the battleground states would not have led to a Clinton victory. The votes are simply not there. To test this theory, Civis Analytics looked at levels of support in high-percentage African-American counties in our five states—Ohio, Pennsylvania, North Carolina, Wisconsin, Michigan—as well as Florida. It categorized high-percentage African-American counties as any county with an African-American population of 25 percent or more. In each of those identified counties, it replaced Clinton and Trump raw votes with Obama and Romney votes, respectively, and calculated the new state-level results.

Out of the six states, only Michigan (16 electoral votes) and Ohio (18) flipped to Clinton. While these two important states would have made the Electoral College count a lot closer (272-266), the national outcome would have remained the same. This research suggests that while African-American turn-out is an important focus, our overall strategy must also include outreach to persuadable white working-class voters. We must reach them in non-urban communities and speak to their unique social and economic anxieties.

To be sure, building capacity and infrastructure to expand African-American voter turnout must be a priority. The issues affecting working families broadly—the economy, education, health care—are acutely felt in the African-American community. These issues, as well as those more specific to people of color, like racial justice, can only be addressed with the robust engagement of African-Americans and other voters of color. In fact, Democrats' electoral efforts would be substantially improved by more investment in political organizing that engaged communities of color at all times, not just in the few months before Election Day. However, reliance on base turnout alone is too narrow of a strategy to win in battleground states and should be augmented.

Why White Working-Class Swing Voters Turned to Trump and What Can Bring Them Back

As noted earlier, Clinton won 1.02 million fewer votes than Obama in the five states we examined. Our analysis of this drop-off found that it was driven largely, but not exclusively, by white Obama voters who swung away from Clinton and who lived disproportionately in non-urban areas. Of this vote loss, 831,082 (81%) came from non-urban counties where the population was considerably whiter than the urban centers.

Having run field canvass programs in Ohio, Pennsylvania and North Carolina in both 2012 and 2016, Working America examined our candidate ID data from 7,531 voters canvassed in both years, focusing on the 4,854 voters who supported Obama. (These IDs were concentrated largely in urban population centers [95%], and are most indicative of the trends in those communities.) This ID data provides more insights into voters who supported Obama in 2012 but ended up backing Trump in 2016.

White voters were more likely than voters of color to defect to Trump in 2016. Of the 3,799 white voters who voted for Obama in 2012 and whom we canvassed in 2016, 28 percent told our canvassers that they were

How White Obama Voters from 2012 Voted in 2016

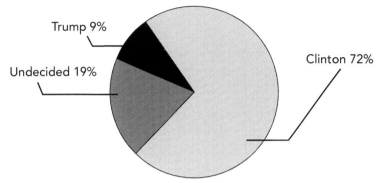

Trump 9%

Undecided 19%

Clinton 72%

Source: 2016 Working America Canvass of White Voters IDed for Obama in 2012.

How Black Obama Voters from 2012 Voted in 2016

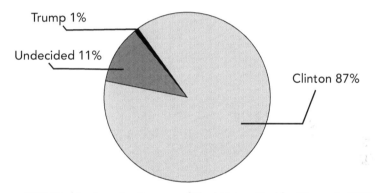

Trump 1%

Undecided 11%

Clinton 87%

Source: 2016 Working America Canvass of Black Voters IDed for Obama in 2012.

undecided or supporting Trump in 2016. However, white voters weren't the only defectors. Of the 1,074 African-American Obama voters canvassed in 2012 and again in 2016, 12 percent were undecided or supporting Trump in 2016.

We also examined early vote records in Ohio, Wisconsin and North Carolina to answer the question: Did 2016 produce a surge in angry white voters supporting Trump?

While we still need the full voter file in several states, the initial evidence from early vote data and, where we have it, the complete 2016 voter file suggests that there was not a determinative surge from new disgruntled white voters, as much as previous voters swinging away from Democrats. We examined what share of voters in urban counties (which tended to support Clinton) and non-urban counties (which tended toward Trump) had cast ballots in 2012 or were new to the 2016 cycle. In this data, the share of new voters in urban counties and non-urban counties was nearly identical to 2012 levels, indicating that much of the change in the electorate was part of the normal churn of new voters participating and former voters dropping out. Using county-level election results, we compared the geographic distribution of new voters and found they were not overwhelmingly more Republican leaning than the existing voters. In North Carolina, for example, the increase in the white share of the electorate was as likely to be in places where Clinton's vote increased as in places where Trump's increased compared to 2012. In Ohio, where turnout was down for white voters, albeit by a lesser amount than for black voters, the new voters were as likely to be in the urban Clinton strongholds as they were to be in non-urban Trump communities.

Taken together, these data points indicate: that a significant number of voters who backed Obama in 2012 did not back Clinton; that these voters were not exclusively white; and that discontented white voters who were not already part of the anticipated electorate were not a critical factor in Trump's victory. It supports the idea that many of the voters lost by Democrats are not racially animated Trump enthusiasts, but working-class people available to be reached by progressives.

These findings jibe with a *recent survey* by Hart Research's Guy Molyneux estimating that across America there are 23 million white working-class moderates who are open to progressive ideas. His research showed that Trump beat Clinton among white working-class conservatives by an overwhelming 85-point margin. But the outcome was much different among white working-class moderates, where Trump won by a smaller 26 percent margin. In 2012, that same group of moderates voted for Mitt Romney over Barack Obama by just 13 percent. Had Hillary Clinton not suffered such a steep drop in support from white working-class moderates, she almost certainly would have won Michigan, Pennsylvania, Ohio and, with those states, the presidency.

III. UNFAIR FIGHT: How Democrats Lost the Media Air War and Their Ground Game Advantage

The shifting communications landscape undoubtedly abetted the outcomes in this election. But Democrats' campaign spending choices were not calibrated to address this changing landscape, especially given the challenges of reaching unsettled white working-class voters in battleground states.

The primary way most voters received information about the election was via cable and broadcast media as well as social media. Trump was the clear beneficiary. Just the difference in total volume of media exposure between Trump and Clinton was larger than all campaign-directed communication (e.g., paid ads, direct mail, field) combined. While campaign-directed communications were ubiquitous on TV and online, a minority of voters in battleground states reported receiving direct contact—mail, canvass visit, phone calls, etc.—down significantly from 2012. These diverging trends—imbalanced media coverage and decreased direct voter contact—were a seismic shift from the 2008 and 2012 elections. As president, Trump inherits an even larger megaphone, and we should anticipate that saturation-level media coverage of him will continue for the next four years. Based on this, we must reconfigure our direct voter contact efforts proportionally.

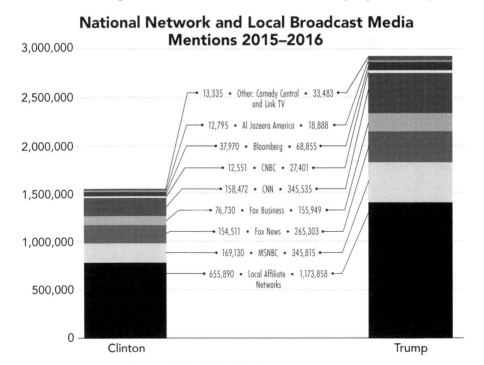

National Network and Local Broadcast Media Mentions 2015–2016

13,335 • Other: Comedy Central and Link TV • 33,483

12,795 • Al Jazeera America • 18,888

37,970 • Bloomberg • 68,855

12,551 • CNBC • 27,401

158,472 • CNN • 345,535

76,730 • Fox Business • 155,949

154,511 • Fox News • 265,303

169,130 • MSNBC • 345,815

655,890 • Local Affiliate Networks • 1,173,858

Source: GDELT Project, Internet Archives Television News

Trump's Unprecedented Advantage in Media Coverage

From the outset, Trump's celebrity drove an outsized advantage in the free media he received from traditional and social media outlets—an advantage over Hillary Clinton of an estimated $2 billion. An analysis by the GDELT Project using data from the Internet Archive's Television News Archives tallied the total mentions that Trump and Clinton received from cable and local broadcast news stations in battleground states. They *found* that Trump garnered 2.28 million TV news (cable and broadcast) mentions vs. 1.27 million for Clinton. The Qatar Computing Research Institute *tallied* candidate traffic on Twitter (retweets, favorability, duration of interests). It found that Trump was three times more popular than Clinton just in the month of October.

While traditional and social media tools had been exploited in previous cycles, it was the celebrity-fueled advantage of Trump that was pervasive and new. While one might expect outlets like Fox News to provide lopsided coverage for Trump vs. Clinton (1.75-to-1 ratio), nominally centrist or liberal outlets like CNN (2.2-to-1), MSNBC (2-to-1) and even local broadcast news (1.79-to-1) were even better for Trump. To understand what drove this dynamic, one need look no further than comments by CNN chief Jeff Zucker on the financial benefit to his network of Trump's blanket coverage—a roughly *$100 million rise in projected* advertising revenue for 2016. Trump figured out early on that ratings drove advertising revenue, which in turn drove coverage volume. As Zucker put it in a forum at the Harvard Institute of Politics, "We put so many [Trump campaign rallies] on because you never knew what he was going to say. They did also attract quite a bit of an audience."

This dramatic imbalance in news coverage was a new phenomenon. Pew's Project for Excellence in Journalism *measured* the volume of news coverage for the major party nominees in both 2008 and 2012, finding that while the tone of coverage varied by party, the volume of coverage was relatively even. While Obama enjoyed slightly more coverage than Romney in the 2012 election, it was a function of stories covering his presidential duties.

Total Presidential Campaign Spending

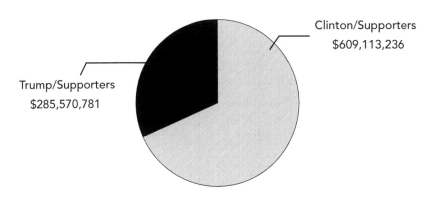

Clinton/Supporters
$609,113,236

Trump/Supporters
$285,570,781

Source: Center for Responsive Politics, 2016 Presidential Race Summary

General Election TV Ad Spending in 2016, Compared to 2012 Spending

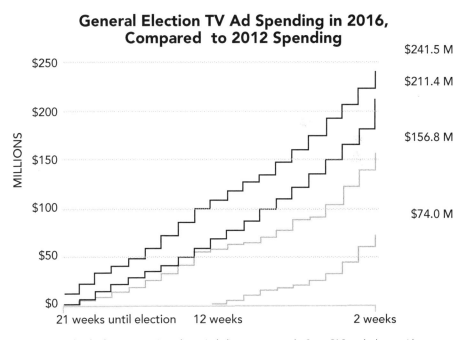

Note: Spending by the two campains only, not including money spent by Super-PACs and other outside groups.
Source: Bloomberg.com 11/2/16 Goldstein, McCormick and Tartar

Clinton's Cash Advantage Didn't Translate into a Ground-Game Advantage

Trump's free media advantage was evident early on, so Clinton's backers were confronted with a question of how to counteract their disadvantage with paid campaign outreach. Here Clinton had a clear war-chest advantage. As one report from on paid media. In just the last four months of the election cycle, Clinton spent $211 million on TV ads in battleground states, almost triple the $74 million spent by Trump—and twice the advantage Obama enjoyed over Mitt Romney in his successful 2012 campaign.

This pattern of robust paid-media spending was consistent with long-standing practice in progressive politics. According to a 2014 article by researchers David Broockman of Stanford University and Josh Kalla of UC Berkeley, the large majority of campaign spending is centered on TV and digital advertising, with only a fraction going to direct voter contact.

The share of investment that did go to direct voter contact was focused to a great extent in the urban population centers, which mostly targeted progressive base voters in the last few months of the campaign. According to one cumulative tracker for the progressive community, 80 percent of all contacts with voters in the five battleground states took place in the urban areas where Clinton did best; 77 percent of contacts targeted Clinton's base, and 83 percent occurred after Labor Day.

The result was that most voters in battleground states did not recall any direct voter contact. According to the national exit polls, only 43 percent of Ohio voters, 38 percent of North Carolina voters and 51 percent of Pennsylvania voters reported receiving direct voter contact from the campaigns or their allies.

Looking at the same question by candidate, 28 percent of Ohio voters said they were contacted by the Clinton campaign vs. 24 percent reporting contact from Trump's. In Pennsylvania, 37 percent of voters said they were contacted by the Clinton campaign compared with 28 percent by Trump. In North Carolina, 26 percent reported contact by the Clinton camp vs. 22

percent by Trump. Despite widespread claims that Trump did not have a ground game, recall of contact from his camp was nearly as large as that from Clinton's. Notably, this level of direct voter contact was down from the 2012 cycle, when 60 percent of battleground state voters reported receiving direct voter contact. That year just over 40 percent of voters in the five battleground states we examined reported receiving direct contact from the Obama camp. Just under 40 percent reported contact from Romney. (Source: "The Ground Game from the Voters Perspective: 2012 and Before," Paul A. Beck and Erik Heidemann)

Given this lack of direct voter contact, the role of paid and earned media took on an even greater significance. It is in this context that the lopsided advantage Trump had in free media became even more important. Clinton and the Democrats made a heavy investment in paid media that targeted base constituencies late in the campaign, but it failed to counter Trump's coverage advantage, the proliferation of "fake news" on the internet and the other novel developments of 2016.

Clearly, the traditional models of campaign communications are no longer adequate to reach the needed voters in the battleground states in an effective way. We propose a different approach.

CONCLUSION:
THE WORKING AMERICA SOLUTION

The systemic losses of the 2016 election reflect a profound failure to establish credibility or connect with voters. We need to make different choices that align with the existing electoral landscape. First, we need to start winning the trust of working-class voters through year-round, in-person engagement. In those conversations and subsequent communications efforts, we need to change the narrative so voters' frustrations are refocused on the appropriate targets instead of on other working-class people who are different from them. By doing so, we can defuse right-wing messages that target "others" and negate demands for racial justice. Instead, we can help unify working people across race, age and gender lines around a common agenda that holds corporate elites accountable for the challenges working people face. And we must do the hard work of stitching back together our communities by anchoring people in organizations that cut across differences to unify around a broad progressive economic agenda. It's work we can do only when we're reaching people in their communities.

Given how consequential the loss of support among working-class voters has been for all progressives, we believe there is an urgency to doing what we know works. Working America's 14 years of organizing working-class voters via face-to-face canvass organizing—doing what *The American Prospect* called "the hardest job in the country" this election cycle—is the basis from which we derive our next steps.

1. **Clearly assess the electoral landscape** for each state and contest. While prevailing in some places may be a matter of turning out Democratic- inclined constituencies, in others the path to success includes reaching and persuading white working-class voters in large population centers and small towns.

Engage voters with high-quality, face-to-face conversations that are as much about listening as talking. It's this kind of organizing that persuades the skeptical and mobilizes the committed. In the last five years, Working America has conducted 50 clinical experiments to evaluate and refine our political program. Lessons from those tests are applicable here. Journalist Andrew Cockburn notes in his April 2016 piece in Harper's

Magazine, "Of all the ways to get people to come out and vote tested by the academics, one emerged as the absolute gold standard. Talking to them face-to-face, the longer the better, turned out to have a dramatic effect.... [T]he effect is infinitely more cost-effective than any traditional media-heavy approach."

Persuasion: In most instances, Working America has had large positive effects on changing the minds of white working-class voters about candidates. However, those positive effects can be highly dependent on timing. For example, early in the 2016 cycle, the Working America canvass had a measurable effect on changing support from Republican to Democratic candidates. In one experiment from Ohio, canvassers in June caused incumbent GOP Sen. Rob Portman's disapproval numbers to increase by 8 points while spurring a corresponding positive effect for Democratic challenger Ted Strickland. These results are consistent with tests in Ohio in the 2012 election cycle, where voters reached by our canvass increased their support for both President Obama and Democratic Sen. Sherrod Brown by 8 points.

However, by September 2016, we saw that the opportunity to move voters had narrowed considerably as they split both for and against Democrats. In tests in Ohio and North Carolina, we found as many voters moving against Clinton and her Democratic Senate ticket-mates as were being persuaded toward them. While these findings were effective for the purpose of focusing the canvass on more productive targets, the range of voters available for persuasion had narrowed considerably.

While the persuasion effects early in the cycle worked broadly among all voters, the diminishing persuasion effects later on resulted in the need for a far more surgical approach to targeting.

Understanding how and when to move voters toward a candidate is useful, but the task before us in future elections will be much different. Instead of moving voters' views of a specific candidate, we must acknowledge the right-wing surround-sound in which voters live and utilize an appropriately scaled response to change the way they interpret the shifting political and economic realities. This objective is much more ambitious than changing a vote for a single election. Fortunately, we have the opportunity to begin this work now in a less crowded information environment and do not have to compete against a clear and aggressively promoted alternative like we do during elections. Investing in year-round, face-to-face engagement also provides an opportunity to educate voters on the decisions of their elected officials at all levels of government that are rarely evident to the average constituent.

Considering that in every community in which Working America has organized, roughly two out of three people we contact become members, we believe there is strong evidence that voters will respond to an issue-based economic argument and be better able to interpret which political candidates align with their interests during election season.

Mobilization: Progressives need to stimulate consistent turnout from base voters, especially in lower-turnout contests like midterm and local elections. While complete 2016 voter file data will not be available for several months, we see strong indications in the early vote data that repeated canvass contact from Working America can drive turnout long term. In North Carolina, for example, voters who were canvassed during the 2014 and 2016 cycles turned out during the voting period at a rate 3 points higher than those canvassed only in 2016. Once the voter file is updated in all of our states, we will have a more complete read of the compounding turnout effects from repeated in-person contact.

This cycle's early analysis follows a nine-state experiment in 2014, where we found that Working America members who were canvassed twice that year (once early in the cycle during issue campaigning and again during the election) turned out at a rate 3.5 points higher than those who were only canvassed once earlier in the year.

The lesson here is that repeated **canvass contact can yield compounding effects on voting behavior, turning people with weaker voting histories into regular likely voters. Both for persuasion and mobilization purposes, we believe that canvass contact of the same individuals multiple times throughout the cycle will build the progressive vote well before cross pressures from a campaign make moving voters harder and costlier.** We must reach big-city and small-town voters, a key part of the combined electorate needed to build progressive power and reach across racial constituencies.

2. **Make measurement and evaluation central** to this longer-term organizing approach. Working America's commitment to learning from clinical measurement has propelled us to understand which parts of our program work and which do not. In 2016, we built on evaluations conducted in previous cycles and established in-house research and opinion survey tools that allowed us to measure change of voter attitudes and the persistence of that change. Our findings suggest that conversations in 2017 can change the way a voter behaves in 2018 and beyond. While there is much evidence to support this thesis, it must be constantly tested and refined so we are certain of the effect before the next election.

3. **Build an alternative communications stream.** Sustaining communication with voters after canvass contact is essential in an environment of fake news and ratings-driven media coverage. The Working America digital communications program fills that need. As part of the issue-organizing and election canvass programs, we regularly collect email addresses from a third of people we canvass. Those email addresses are then folded into the Working America member communications program.

4. As effective as email communication plans have been at generating online activism and in some instances raising money, we worked this cycle to answer the nagging question of how the digital channel can be used to change voter choices and behavior. In clinical tests in North Carolina and Ohio Supreme Court elections—low-profile contests where one in four voters did not traditionally cast ballots—we measured large effects (+21 points and +14 points, respectively) on getting voters who backed Clinton to support a down-ticket candidate. The communications treatment in these tests differed from the standard email program. We anchored the weeklong treatment with saturation-level emails about the candidates that highlighted issues that resonated with voters. Those emails were reinforced by social media ads keyed to the email address. A small segment of the recipients also received text messages. Not only were the effects large, but they were universal. For example, in North Carolina, white voters increased their support at the same rate as black voters for Michael Morgan, an African-American judge recently elected to the state's high

court. As part of this long-term organizing effort, our member communications strategy can also move voters on low-profile issues that may not be closely followed. For example, the evening news rarely reports on proposals to repeal new federal overtime regulations or limit the Consumer Financial Protection Board's power to curb abusive banking practices, but these actions profoundly affect the economic lives of the working class. Our member communications program can deliver regular information on these issues that is easily digested by the recipient—all at a relatively low cost. This issue awareness would then be the context in which future candidates for office are judged.

5. **Create community.** As effective as canvass contact and member communications can be, we believe that a segment of voters are looking for a continuing presence—a place to go, to talk and to act. There are numerous progressive organizations with effective models for community organizing, although very few focus on working-class suburban, exurban and small-town populations. The Working America model of developing multiracial teams of activists is one approach. For example, our community team in Greensboro, N.C., which engages about 100 local activists, has led the way on providing paid family leave and increasing the minimum wage to $15 per hour for municipal employees. There are a number of approaches we can take, but the need for sustained community engagement to cultivate activists is apparent. We believe this work will require a large-scale engagement between 2017 and 2020, with constant reassessments along the way.

6. Starting in early 2017, we need to begin hiring and training large teams of canvass organizers, including many of the seasoned organizers from the 2016 cycle. In our experience, effective organizing is a skill that requires time and practice to develop. We will use the first six months of this year to build the proficiency of the canvass staff and experiment with organizing, educating and persuading many of the disaffected voters we lost this year. Our work will cover the large urban population centers and smaller towns that have received less direct contact from progressives.

During this initial period, we will also conduct clinical experiments in the field that measure issue and partisan persuasion. We'll test which voters are most responsive, for how long and in what context. In the second half of 2017, we will focus the work on off-year elections—largely special elections and local contests such as municipal races in Ohio and legislative contests in North Carolina. In addition to increasing the odds of winning, this will yield important information, such as: How many contacts does it take to change the partisan and issue orientation of a voter? What is the right combination of in-person and digital communications to fortify a voter against political cross pressure? And what is the maximum degree of effectiveness a canvasser can attain via persuasion?

7. Drawing from the lessons of 2017, we will then begin to scale up the canvass staff ahead of the 2018 elections, continuing to test and adjust the program as we progress. Presumably, much of the issue campaigning of 2017-18 will be calibrated to help these voters under-stand the decisions of incumbent policymakers from a progressive perspective. The work needs to fortify voters against the continuous drumbeat of Trump-dominated media and the inevitable onslaught of campaign communications. Our goal in this two-year period is to deliver significant wins for progressive candidates by the end of 2018, building momentum toward 2020. Based on what is learned from the first cycle, we will chart the path for the following two years.

A TALE OF TWO POPULISMS
Guy Molyneux

Many analysts, and leading Democrats, have attributed Donald Trump's impressive 2016 vote margin among white working class voters to his embrace of economic populism. In the wake of Trump's victory, Senator Bernie Sanders suggested that, "millions of Americans registered a protest vote on Tuesday, expressing their fierce opposition to an economic and political system that puts wealthy and corporate interests over their own. Donald J. Trump won the White House because his campaign rhetoric successfully tapped into a very real and justified anger, an anger that many traditional Democrats feel."

Senator Elizabeth Warren also identified possible common ground on economic issues: "When President- elect Trump wants to take on these issues, when his goal is to increase the economic security of the middle-class families, then count me in."

Democrats can take obvious comfort in a story about Trump winning in large measure because he stole our ideas. And

Also by Guy Molyneux:

White Working Class Moderates—A critical group of "persuadable" white working Americans.

In a widely quoted article in the Winter American Prospect, Guy Molyneux presents data to show that there is a critically important subset of white working-class moderates. These "persuadable" white working class voters represent about 35 of white working Americans and 15 percent of the overall electorate. Molyneux evaluates which issues and proposals best appeal to this critical group.

http://prospect.org/article/mapping-white-working-class

Guy Molyneux is a partner with Hart Research Associates

there may be strategic value in this argument for Democratic leaders, who hope either to nudge Trump in a progressive direction or—more plausibly—lay the groundwork for accusing him of breaking promises when he fails to do so. When Democratic Leader Chuck Schumer says, "President Trump ran as a populist and still talks like one, but his first month has been a boon for corporations, the wealthy and elite in America," he is trying to box Trump in and start developing a 2018 campaign message.

However, as an analysis of why so many white non-college voters pulled the lever for Trump, this assessment misses the mark in important ways. In order to develop strategies for winning back these voters, it's important to get the story right. Trump's populism surely played a role in the surge of white working class voters to the GOP ticket in 2016. But Trump's populism—and more importantly, that of working-class whites—differs in important ways from the populism of Bernie Sanders and Elizabeth Warren. I don't mean only that Trump's populism incorporates racial grievance and crude nationalism, though that is clearly a critical distinction both morally and politically. Even setting aside Trump's ethnonationalism, these two populisms have less in common than it may appear.

Bernie Sanders and Elizabeth Warren are the champions of what we can call economic populism, a worldview centered on contrasting the interests of working people with those of economic elites. In Warren's now famous formulation, the system is rigged:

> People feel like the system is rigged against them. And here's the painful part: they're right. The system is rigged. Look around. Oil companies guzzle down billions in subsidies. Billionaires pay lower tax rates than their secretaries. Wall Street CEOs—the same ones who wrecked our economy and destroyed millions of jobs—still strut around Congress, no shame, demanding favors, and acting like we should thank them.

For economic populists, the bad guys are the wealthy, corporations, and CEOs—with a special place in Hell reserved for Wall Street. Donald Trump, however, tells a fundamentally different story about how the world works, and who has been winning and losing. Here is Trump's version of populism, as expressed in his inaugural address:

> For too long, a small group in our nation's Capital has reaped the rewards of government while the people have borne the cost.

Washington flourished—but the people did not share in its wealth. Politicians prospered—but the jobs left, and the factories closed. The establishment protected itself, but not the citizens of our country. Their victories have not been your victories; their triumphs have not been your triumphs; and while they celebrated in our nation's Capital, there was little to celebrate for struggling families all across our land.

Warren speaks of the power of economic elites to further enrich themselves at the expense of average people. But in Trump's story, it is *political* elites who wear the black hats. This is political populism: the people have been betrayed by their government.

Progressives mock Trump for claiming he wants to "drain the swamp" while promising to deliver deregulation, regressive tax cuts, and other goodies to special interests. But in Trump's view, the "swamp" is filled with bureaucrats, not billionaires. His answer to "corruption" is to rescind civil service protections for federal workers, not limit political spending. His political reform agenda consists almost entirely of telling *politicians* what they cannot do—banning lobbying by former members of Congress and executive branch officials—rather than restricting powerful interests.

It is true that Trump has embraced some economic ideas that depart from traditional Republican free-market orthodoxy, most obviously his hostility toward free trade agreements. But even on the trade issue, where the two populisms converge most closely, they offer distinct narratives. Compare Bernie Sanders and Trump:

SANDERS: I voted against NAFTA, CAFTA, PNTR with China. I think they have been a disaster for the American worker. A lot of corporations that shut down here move abroad.... TPP was written by corporate America and the pharmaceutical industry and Wall Street. That's what this trade agreement is about.

TRUMP: For too long, Americans have been forced to accept trade deals that put the interests of insiders and the Washington elite over the hard-working men and women of this country. As a result, blue-collar towns and cities have watched their factories close and good-paying jobs move overseas, while Americans face a mounting trade deficit and a devastated manufacturing base.

Trump does tap into blue collar whites' worries about job loss and stagnation in declining manufacturing communities, but note who benefits: not multinational corporations or their CEOs, but the "Washington elite." Sanders speaks of corporations moving overseas, but in Trump's trade narrative it is the "jobs" that move, and the bad actors once again are politicians (and the foreign countries that take advantage of their incompetence). In political populism, corporate interests and the wealthy remain invisible. Indeed, one might even say that is its primary purpose.

Trump's political populism is, fundamentally, a story about the failure of government. And unfortunately, there is good reason to believe it deeply resonates with white working class voters. Just 20 percent of them believe they can trust the federal government more than half of the time (a rather low bar). While 61 percent of white working class voters have an unfavorable view of corporations, a stratospheric 93 percent have an unfavorable view of politicians. Given a choice between positive and negative statements about government's capacity and performance, white non-college voters consistently pick the negative view:

38 percent chose: "We need a government that does more to solve problems and help people."
62 percent chose: "We need a government that is smaller, less expensive, and interferes less in people's lives."

32 percent chose: "When government tries to solve a problem, it usually does more good than harm."
68 percent chose: "When government tries to solve a problem, it usually does more harm than good."

27 percent chose: "Government has helped me achieve my goals."
73 percent chose: "Government has made it harder for me to achieve my goals."

This anti-government sentiment is mainly driven by antipathy toward political leaders, rather than governmental agencies and departments. When white non-college voters think about the government in Washington, 83 percent say they think first about elected officials, while just 17 percent say that programs and agencies are what first come to mind.

In focus groups, I conducted with white working class voters last year for Americans for a Fair Deal, it was clear that confidence in politicians and the political system was virtually non-existent. Among the comments:

"They put their political career first. It seems like it's all self-interest in government. It's they're never agreeable on anything. It's always what is about them."

"Everybody that's in the government is a lawyer. They're from a very well-to-do family. They've always had everyone doing things for them, and they're like the silver-spoon-in-their-mouth kind of scenario. So they've never struggled. They don't really understand the little people like the average American, because they're not average Americans."

We asked our focus group participants what they want from their political leaders, and the answers are revealing. They did not talk about jobs, or trade deals, or any other policy goal. Again and again, they told us they just want leaders who care about the people and not only themselves.

"Focus on the needs of the people not special interests."

"Care more about the people they represent and less about the office they hold."

"Have the best interests of the common American in mind."

"Care about the people of the country instead of making their wallets bigger."

This distrust of government is, by far, the least appreciated factor underlying Trump's 2016 victory. Much of the post-election analysis has debated whether Trump's appeal was three parts economic populism to two parts racism, or 70-30 the other way, when hostility to politicians and government was likely just as important as either of these other two factors.

Political distrust has developed over decades, and has many causes. But let us give the devil his due, and acknowledge that Mitch McConnell, more than any other single person, is the father of Trumpism. By grinding Washington to a virtual halt for years, his blanket opposition to

Obama helped ratchet up public disgust with the federal government to previously unseen heights. Even while the economy was recovering, confidence in Washington fell steadily, an impressive if perverse feat.

In such a climate, the appeal of an outsider like Donald Trump is readily apparent, as is the enormous handicap imposed on Hillary Clinton, who was perceived by much of the public as the nearly perfect embodiment of "career politician." White working class voters did not fear electing someone with no political experience, because those with experience had so clearly failed. Warnings of Trump's unfitness for office from institutions that historically play a vetting role in our political system, such as newspaper editorial boards, were largely disregarded because the "experts" had gotten so much else wrong.

While particularly well suited to the conditions of 2016, the threat posed by Trump's political populism continues. As a means of winning white working class votes, it represents a quantum leap forward for Republicans. The small government vision of Paul Ryan had limited appeal to these voters, and that remains true even while their anger at government has grown. Non-college whites believe government has let them down, but most have no principled or ideological objections to government playing a strong role in the economy. Although just 20 percent trust the federal government, 50 percent also say it should take a more active role in solving the nation's economic and social problems. Indeed, two-thirds (68 percent) say the federal government should do more to create jobs and improve wages, and majorities also say it should do more to improve K-12 education, make college affordable, and regulate banks and the financial sector.

Trump's political populism is more compelling to these voters than Ryan's small government message because it is less abstract and ideological. It speaks to their economic concerns in a powerful way and provides a plausible explanatory narrative: Americans are struggling because they have been betrayed by their political leaders, and taken advantage of by foreign nations. Of course, Trump also is also careful not to threaten their Social Security and Medicare benefits, no small thing.

While the anti-government sentiment that Trump exploits and encourages may differ in important respects from Ryan's vision, functionally it poses many of the same challenges for progressives. White working-class voters' negative view of government spending undermines their potential support for many progressive economic policies. While they want something done about jobs, wages, education, and healthcare, they are also fiscally conservative and deeply skeptical of government's ability to make positive change. So political populism not only differs from economic populism, but also serves as a powerful barrier to it.

Looking forward, progressives must find ways to puncture the belief of working class whites that Trump is delivering a government "controlled by the people." Many Democrats hope that Trump's cabinet of billionaires has begun undermining his populist credentials. Each successive appointment was met with howls that he was betraying his promises to the working class. But if billionaires were anathema to Trump's white working class supporters, they probably wouldn't have elected one to the presidency. They wanted to kick out the career politicians and try something different, and Trump's reliance on CEOs and military generals has largely honored that wish. The lack of government experience in Trump's administration may frighten many Democrats, but in the eyes of his followers it's the best recommendation imaginable.

My guess is that Trump will lose ground if and when white working class voters see that he is not delivering for them, and is in fact serving others. Democrats must aggressively contest Trump's core promise to the white working class: that he is putting the government to work for them. Much of Trump's actual agenda is of course devoted to helping millionaires and large corporations. Our job is to make it impossible for working class Americans to miss, or deny, that reality.

We don't know yet which issues will provide the best openings for accomplishing that task. Republicans' as yet unsuccessful assaults on Medicaid and the Affordable Care Act, and their ongoing attacks on food stamps, workplace safety, financial regulation, and many other protections for working people all represent policy catastrophes, but also potential political opportunities.

One issue that particularly engages the working class is also at the top of Republicans' agenda: taxes. Working-class voters are passionate in their insistence that wealthy individuals and large corporations are not paying their fair share, and efforts to give new tax cuts to those at the top will meet with strong resistance. In a recent poll my firm conducted for the Center for American Progress in 2018 Senate battleground states, 54 percent of white working class voters had an unfavorable reaction to GOP plans to pass across-the-board cuts in tax rates that would give a large tax cut to millionaires, and 52 percent objected to large rate cuts for corporations. If Trump delivers huge tax cuts to corporations and the wealthy, he will shake the faith of many of his blue-collar supporters.

In terms of a broader message, Democrats' traditional economic populism offers a starting point, but we need to also borrow a bit from Trump's playbook. We must speak not only about inequality and unfairness in our economy, but also about politicians who use their political power on behalf of corporations and the wealthy. White working class voters are less interested in cutting down the size of government (38 percent) than intaking back their government so that it works for all Americans (62 percent). In another survey we conducted for CAP, we identified a particularly powerful way of articulating that idea from a progressive perspective:

> We need to take back our government so that it works for all Americans, not just billionaires and special interests. The size of government is less important than who it works for. Instead of giving tax breaks and subsidies to big corporations, we should create jobs, improve education, lift wages, and help people retire with dignity. And we should get big money out of politics, so that our government is accountable to the people.

By 64 percent to 36 percent, our white working class respondents reported they would vote for a candidate with this message over a conservative candidate promising to cut government waste and "revive the American dream by curbing big government."

Steve Bannon and his team will work hard to keep Trump's political outsider brand alive. Ongoing wars with the mainstream media and the federal bureaucracy will give the story some plausibility, and they will enjoy plenty of air cover from the Fox/Breitbart propaganda machine. Still, it will become increasingly hard for Trump, now that he's president, to pose as the slayer of "political elites." He runs the government now, and campaigning against Washington will increasingly seem more like ducking responsibility than brave truth telling.

Moreover, Democrats can assign clear responsibility for every shortcoming of the federal government to what Paul Ryan helpfully calls our "unified Republican government." Republicans control every branch of the government, and they will own what they break. The message task for Democrats is to identify the underlying problem not as "politicians" generically, but those politicians who rule on behalf of millionaires and corporate titans. We now have a tremendous opportunity to leverage public disgust with government, while focusing it on its proper target: Republicans' determination to use government power to enrich the rich and empower the powerful.

SOURCES:
1. Hart Research national survey on trust in government, conducted for CAP, August 2015.
2. Hart Research survey in 2018 Senate battleground states, conducted for CAP, December 2016.
3. Focus groups with white non-college voters in Alabama, Pennsylvania, Tennessee, and Wisconsin, conducted for Americans for a Fair Deal in April and May, 2016.

THE DEMOCRATIC PARTY AND THE WHITE WORKING CLASS
Celinda Lake , Daniel Gotoff, and Olivia Myszkowski

The challenge Democrats face today—uniting a broad coalition of working class Americans that spans racial, regional, gender, and generational lines—is far from new, but it has not always been this daunting. Following a period in which white working class voters helped deliver victories for a generation under Presidents Roosevelt and Truman, this bloc has proven elusive to Democrats in the modern era of political campaigns, going back at least four decades and perhaps more. In the 1992 Presidential race and again in 1996, Bill Clinton beat his Republican rivals among white non-college educated voters, in each instance with a plurality and by one point.[1] In 1992, it was the first time in at least twelve years that a Democratic Presidential candidate had won this demographic group, and since Clinton's reelection in '96, non-college educated white voters have consistently evaded the grasp of the Democratic Party. While Donald Trump's sweeping victory with these voters this past November represents a widened gulf between the voting patterns of college educated and non-college educated whites (Trump won the former group by 4 points, and the latter by

Also By Celinda Lake:

Strategic Analysis: The Post Election Environment

Democratic Pollster Celinda Lake and her associates analyze a wide range of opinion polls on attitudes toward Donald Trump, the GOP, Bernie Sanders and Barack Obama in the aftermath of the election with the goal of defining new strategies for the future. The analysis examines Obama's post election popularity and its implications for successful Democratic resistance to the conservative agenda.

https://mediarelations.gwu.edu/ sites/mediarelations.gwu.edu/ files/GWBattlegroundPoll61- demmemo.pdf

Celinda Lake is a partner in Lake Research Partners

---

[1]Montanaro, D. 7 Reasons Donald Trump Won The Presidential Election. November 12, 2016.

39),[2] the Democratic Party's problems with the white working class are neither new nor unique to 2016. However, neither are efforts—like this commendable undertaking—to analyze the challenge and devise a solution. While individual proposals for reform may test well with voters, these ideas alone are not enough. To meaningfully re-engage the white working class with the Democratic Party's agenda, a coherent, compelling narrative about how our platform provides genuine solutions to economic problems is of critical importance.

November's staggering results are a reminder to Democrats that the racially diverse, young, educated, unmarried (women) and urban voters who comprised a significant portion of the Obama Coalition do not constitute an inexorable path to Electoral College victory for Democrats. In 2008 and 2012, Barack Obama consolidated the Rising American Electorate (RAE), but also captured critical majorities in places like Sawyer County, Wisconsin; Luzerne County, Pennsylvania; and Macomb County, Michigan—all home to significant numbers of white working class voters. These were just three of the 219 counties that flipped from Obama in 2012 to Trump in 2016.[3]

White working class voters in these parts of the country, former hubs of manufacturing and production, feel economically abandoned by both parties in Washington, D.C.—reeling not just from the effects of an increasingly globalized economy that has traded American jobs for corporate profits made on the backs of cheap overseas labor, but also by a political establishment in the nation's capital that they see as more interested in rewarding wealthy campaign benefactors, and the industries and interests they represent, at the expense of ordinary Americans. Indeed, a CNN/ORC poll conducted in February of 2016 showed that the vast majority of Americans believe that the U.S. economic system generally favors the wealthy (71 percent) instead of being fair to most Americans (27 percent).[4] The idea that income and wealth should be more evenly distributed among Americans has won the

---

[2]Ibid.
[3]Taylor, J. The Counties That Flipped From Obama To Trump, In 3 Charts. November 15, 2016.
[4]CNN/ORC Poll. February 24-27, 2016.
[5]CBS News Poll. July 29-August 2, 2015, July 11-16, 2012

support of 60 percent or greater since 2012[5], but Americans are skeptical that government officials will act to protect their best interests. According to a 2015 Gallup report, 75 percent of Americans perceive corruption as widespread in the country's government.[6]

Not only have Democrats presided in Washington for significant stretches while these trends have developed; they have, in visible ways, exacerbated those trends, through, for instance, global trade deals enacted in the 1990's and the repeal of Glass-Steagall. This is certainly not to blame the Democratic Party for all the ills that have been inflicted on the country over the past 40 years, far from it. But too many times, our Party has been guilty not just of sins of omission—failing to stand up to the Republicans on critical issues, or even providing the GOP cover in some cases (with some congressional Democrats supporting the Bush tax cuts and the war in Iraq)—but of commission, too. The Obama administration's embrace of the financial industry early in his first term, combined with the decision not to prosecute any of the individuals and institutions responsible for the economic collapse of 2008, led to a new low point in the Democratic Party's image as a formidable check on Wall Street. In the 2010 midterm elections, voters who blamed Wall Street for the country's economic problems preferred Republican candidates by a margin of 16 points, despite the Democratic Party's efforts to deliver a message against Wall Street special interests.[7]

Given this reality, it is not particularly surprising that the Party has as yet been unable to articulate a clear, credible, and commanding vision for the economic revitalization of the country, the middle class, and specifically the hollowed-out communities in which many white working class voters struggle. The white working class's sense of its economic isolation is compounded by a gap in cultural sensibilities; white working class voters, particularly baby boomers and older, tend to be less liberal on social issues than their more educated (and more urban) counterparts, whose support has been nurtured by the Democratic Party for the

[6]Gallup. 75% in U.S. See Widespread Government Corruption. September 19, 2015.
[7]National Election Pool Exit Report. 2010.

past several election cycles. Among college-educated whites, Democrats are faring better. Trump outperformed Hillary Clinton among college educated white voters by 4 points in 2016, a much smaller margin than Mitt Romney's 14-point edge over Barack Obama in 2012.[8] Far from being a call for Democrats to moderate their stance on such issues as a woman's right to choose, gun safety reforms, and equal protection of civil rights for all Americans, our point is that when Democrats fail to offer a compelling economic vision and agenda, the opposition not only benefits from that failure, but is allowed the opportunity to shift the debate to areas where it enjoys greater advantages over Democrats. In a political environment where Republicans have shifted the terms of debate to stoke racist biases (nearly half of Trump's supporters describe African Americans as more "violent" than whites[9]) and sexist inclinations (67 percent of Trump supporters deny the role of sexism in America[10]), the need for a forceful, serious, policy-and values-driven Democratic platform has never been greater.

Recent face-to-face conversations with working class voters in Florida, Missouri, North Carolina, Ohio, and Pennsylvania conducted by Working America[11] in the weeks following the election underscore the intense economic anxiety that pervades their communities and their lives. Working class Trump and Clinton voters alike reported that they want the President-elect to address jobs and the economy first, with Trump voters expressing more urgency (37 percent say that the economy and jobs are the most important issue, compared to 21 percent of Clinton voters). For some white working class Trump voters, their perception of the candidate's focus on bringing jobs back to their communities took priority over their serious misgivings about him. As one white working class Trump voter from the Pittsburgh area told Working America: "Trump's an asshole. But sometimes you need an asshole to make things better and shake things up."[12] Both Obama in 2008 and Trump in 2016 tapped into an intense desire for change and spoke to pervasive economic anxieties; this thematic commonality helps to explain the crossover appeal of two otherwise disparate

[8]Montanaro, D. 7 Reasons Donald Trump Won The Presidential Election. November 12, 2016.
[9]Flitter, E., & Kahn, C. Exclusive: Trump supporters more likely to view blacks negatively - Reuters/Ipsos poll. June 28, 2016.
[10]Pew Research Poll. June 7-July 5, 2016.
[11]Working America. Front Porch Focus Group Report. January 2017.
[12]Ibid.

politicians for some white working class voters. Research in the weeks immediately following Trump's inauguration showed that white, blue-collar Trump supporters were particularly impressed by the speed at which the Trump administration had been implementing the President's campaign agenda.[13]

For the last several election cycles, we have urged the Democrats to develop a strong vision for the American economy that addresses the deep-rooted concerns of the working class and provides solutions to the scope of the challenges we face. Trump's ascent to power even though he was the most disliked president candidate in history, on the strength of a white working class supermajority, reminds us that this bold economic message and policy agenda is more important now than ever.

That said, given the Democratic Party's historic deficits with this demographic group, it is unlikely—and frankly, unrealistic—that Democrats will be able to make up all the ground that has been lost with white working class voters by 2018 or even 2020. As such, the Democratic Party's efforts should be structured specifically to engage the white working class voters that Obama won in 2008 and 2012 that Clinton then lost in 2016—the voters living in swing counties like Sawyer, Luzerne, and Macomb. It should also be noted that we believe such efforts must not come at the expense of (re)engaging the significant swaths of the country who do not regularly turn out to vote, whose patterns of voting are irregular, and/or who no longer feel a sense of loyalty to the Democrats; we look forward to that discussion as well.

According to estimates by the *New York Times*[14] and *The New Republic*[15], the election was lost for Clinton by between 77,000 and 110,000 votes in Michigan, Pennsylvania, and Wisconsin. Making up this particular difference will be key if the Democrats are to build back from what is a historic nadir of political power at all levels of government today. To do this, the Democratic Party requires a robust economic vision that appeals to the appetite for populist reform; a forceful push-back against Trumpian policies that hurt working Americans; and a

---

[13]Lake Research Partners Focus Groups. February 2017.
[14]Burns, J. M. Democrats at Crossroads: Win Back Working-Class Whites, or Let Them Go? December 15, 2016.
[15]Vyse, G. With a White Working-Class Focus, Are Democrats Going Back to the '90s? November 21, 2016.

commitment to campaign finance reform and removing the influence of big money in elections, which voters believe is the first step to implementing economic—and other types of needed—change.

Indeed, in order to reposition itself as the party of all working Americans, bold economic proposals will not be enough for Democrats. The Democratic Party's historic strength, dating back to the New Deal, has been to offer a vision of government that actively works to protect working people and makes their lives better. A central appeal of the current economic populist agenda focuses on the importance of limiting the power of big money in politics. Especially in the aftermath of the Citizens United ruling, there exists substantial political will among Americans of both parties to restrict the influence of the hyper wealthy when it comes to campaign donations.[16] In fact, a February 2016 poll conducted by Rasmussen Research found that 76 percent of Americans believe that the wealthiest individuals and companies have too much power and influence over elections—that majority holds across gender, age, race, and party lines.[17] Our own research in 2011 found that, above all other regulations, voters are interested in government oversight of the relationship between special interests and politicians (77 percent)[18]. A populist economic message is especially powerful when it hinges on a greater push for reform; by utilizing this frame, the Democratic Party may be able to draw contrasts that blunt the appeal of populism on the Right.

At a time where billionaires, Wall Street executives, and other titans of industry now occupy the White House, the contrast between the power exercised by the elite and that of working-class Americans has never been starker. Through political maneuvering and diversion, Donald Trump was able to frame his candidacy as a siren call to the white working class. But now that he's President, all of the pieces are in place for the Democratic Party to turn this message back against him. Part of that push-back should be grounded in clear, broadly disseminated articulations of how his administration's actions are hurting all working class Americans. Additionally, however, the

---

[16]Thee-Brenan, N. C. Poll Shows Americans Favor an Overhaul of Campaign Financing. June 2, 2015.
[17]Rasmussen Poll. February 9-10, 2016.
[18]Lake Research Partners. OMB Watch Report. 2011.

Democrats face the real challenge of embodying the values of working Americans through its leadership, its professed values, the scope of its policy agenda, and its commitment to action. This will mean purposefully cultivating and supporting candidates who resonate with working class Americans even though they lack the financial heft that has characterized the prototypical Democratic candidate in recent years.

A Bold Economic Vision

As the Party seeks to make inroads with white working class voters, Democrats' strength can come from the existing popularity of policy reforms that advance a progressive economic agenda. This will mean forcefully defining the Party's platform in places where we failed in 2016; in our post-election work thus far, we've found that even Clinton voters have struggled to identify the Democratic Party's vision for the country's future. As Democrats offer bolder policy alternatives, it will be especially important for the Party to draw pointed contrasts to Trump and gain an edge from his administration's inability to deliver on promises for a better economy with good-paying jobs. The Democratic Party's power in 2018 and beyond will be contingent, in part, on our ability to articulate Trump's failure to "make America great", and the administration's real consequences for working people.

A national survey conducted in 2015 for the Progressive Change Institute explored the public's appetite for a number of far-reaching economic reforms, and found strong enthusiasm from the majority of voters. A proposal to institute fair trade that protects workers, the environment, and jobs enjoyed the support of 75 percent of voters.[19] Similarly, more than seven-in-ten voters (71 percent) supported a Medicare buy-in for all Americans; a Full Employment Act (70 percent support); a Green New Deal- and major infrastructure- jobs programs (70 percent support each); taxing the rich at the same higher rate that President Reagan did (59 percent support); and breaking up the big banks (59 percent support)[20]. Our own research has shown that support for strengthening—and expanding— Social Security and Medicare will

[19]GBA Strategies/Progressive Change Institute Poll. January 9-15, 2015.
[20]Ibid.
[21]Lake Research Partners/NCPSSM Poll. January 4-8, 2017.
[22]Ibid.

also be particularly important, especially giving the relatively advanced age of the 2018 midterm electorate.[21]

Widespread and intense support for such economic reforms (the aforementioned are but a handful of examples) is buttressed by similar public support for policies aimed at giving ordinary Americans a voice in their government again: a proposal to end gerrymandering receives support from 73 percent of voters; public matching for small dollar donations receives support from 57 percent of voters, and full disclosure of corporate spending on politics and lobbying receives support from 71 percent of voters.[22] The demographic breakouts for this poll have not been made available to the public, but given the overall popularity of these proposals, we can extrapolate that they have broad appeal across the electorate, including among white working class voters. Again, a laundry list of popular policy prescriptions do not a winning economic message make, yet these results suggest that the time has come to structure the Democratic Party's agenda around robust reforms—on dimensions of significant economic *and* political change.

Building political support is partly the work of effective messaging. Our polling has shown that when we describe economic conditions through the lens of lived experience—"can't make ends meet" or "can't pull ahead no matter how hard they try"—instead of through abstractions, voters listen and often move to our side. Being explicit about causes of economic harm by referring to CEOs and other leaders provides clarity and generates support for our message, as well.

In many ways, the path forward for rebuilding the Democratic Party's relationship with the white working class was articulated best and most recently by Senator Bernie Sanders' presidential campaign. Sanders' message centered on unabashed economic populism and a commitment to remove the influence of big corporate money from our politics—and hence, our government. This message has also been championed by Elizabeth Warren, Elijah Cummings, and the Congressional Progressive Caucus, as well. Indeed, the latest GWU Battleground Poll suggests that Senator Sanders remains well positioned to serve as a source of strength and leadership. A solid majority (56 percent) of voters hold a positive opinion of him—a higher favorability rating than those of the other national leaders tested in the poll. While non-college educated white voters are split in their view of Sanders (40 percent favorable, 39 percent unfavorable), he far out-performs the Democrats' 2016 Presidential nominee as well as the image of the Party as a whole among those voters, as well as across the board. Again, we must remind ourselves that the (near-term) objective is not win over majorities of these voters; it is to improve—and measurably so—on their declining support for Democrats in recent elections.

Sanders' primary election successes in the states and counties that flipped from Obama victories in 2012 to Trump victories in 2016 further under-score the appeal of his refreshingly progressive message and agenda, espe-cially as we look toward targeting these swing votes in upcoming elections. In Wisconsin, for example, 21 counties that Barack Obama won in 2012 voted for Donald Trump in 2016. Every single one of those 21 counties were won by Bernie Sanders in the April 2016 Wisconsin Democratic Pri-mary, which Sanders won outright and handily. In the Michigan Primary, which Sanders won narrowly, nine of the twelve counties that flipped from Obama to Trump were won by Sanders as well. Obviously, there are nu-merous problems in comparing white working class Democratic Primary voters to white working class General Election voters. Yet, this is far from the only evidence pointing to Sanders' appeal among white working class independents, many of whom he successfully encouraged to join the ranks of the Democratic Party by participating in the 2016 primaries. In a head-to-head matchup between Sanders and Trump in our own April 2016 Bat-tleground survey, Sanders bested Trump 51 percent to 40 percent—though among white non-college graduates, Trump beat Sanders 49 percent to 41 percent[23]

While Sanders' personal popularity and influence is an important take-away from these data, the broader, more salient point that emerges is that the Democratic Party stands to gain politically when it returns its focus to issues of class, including the substantial and ongoing challenges of income inequality and the negative influence of corporate special interests on the lives of working class Americans of all kinds.

Effectively engaging the white working class is an essential task for the Democratic Party, but we must also acknowledge that this work will go to

[23]Lake Research Partners/Tarrance Group Poll. April 2016.

waste if we ignore our base. We believe that the approaches outlined above can serve to energize the base as well as engage the white working class, and should be employed with that goal in mind. By moving forward with an agenda that explicitly continues our commitment to racial and gender justice and opportunities for all, including immigrants, we will work to ensure that our base carries our progressive message into the future.

The path forward will not be easy, but neither is it as mystifying as some may imagine. A sweeping platform of economic and political change resonates powerfully with both the white working class voters that the Democratic Party must attract, as well as the base of the Party (young, diverse, educated, and urban) that Democrats must nurture and energize if it hopes to be successful in the 2018 midterms and the 2020 elections (which will determine the composition of the districts in which we will have to compete for the following decade}. And yet, embracing this change will require not just political smarts, but political will. The Democratic base will need either to convince Party's establishment of the necessity of this approach—or failing that, actively work to replace it. For the Democratic Party, the stakes have never been higher and the challenges have never been clearer.

THE RACISM OBSTACLE
There are limits to how effectively a progressive populist economics can woo working class whites

Joan Walsh

Neither will like the comparison, but it's inescapable. Since the 2016 presidential election, Senator Bernie Sanders sounds like an earlier leader who wanted to overhaul the Democratic Party after a devastating loss: former Arkansas Governor Bill Clinton. Almost 30 years ago, Clinton, like Sanders, struggled to find a way to win back the White House by attracting more white non-college educated voters, the backbone of the New Deal coalition, many of whom had left the party at least partly out of discomfort with the dominance of women and people of color in the Democratic coalition.

LATEST BOOK

JOAN WALSH
EDITOR AT LARGE, SALON.COM, and MSNBC POLITICAL ANALYST
★ ★ ★
WHAT'S THE MATTER WITH WHITE PEOPLE?

FINDING OUR WAY
★ IN THE ★
NEXT AMERICA

"A must-read. Engaging, thoughtful, provocative, utterly persuasive."
—CHRIS MATTHEWS

Clinton promoted his humble origins, and so does Sanders. "I come from the white working class, and I am deeply humiliated that the Democratic Party cannot talk to where I came from," Sanders declared in a speech soon after the shattering election loss to Donald Trump.

Also by Joan Walsh:

Can the Democrats Win Back White Working-Class Voters?

In an important September, 2016 article in the Nation magazine, Walsh discusses whether democrats will be able to win back white working class voters with a range of Democratic political experts that included Joel Benenson, Ruy Teixeira and Karen Nussbaum. She analyzes the views of Thomas Frank and others who, she argued, pay too little attention to the five decade "Southern Strategy" in shaping white workers contemporary views.

https://www.thenation.com/article/can-the-democrats-win-back-white-working-class-voters/

Joan Walsh is a National Affairs Correspondent for The Nation

At this point, the two men's paths diverge. Where Bill Clinton embraced a neoliberal "Third Way," playing down the party's advocacy of government, which had come to be seen as the province of black people and women by those defecting white workers, Sanders seeks a "Third Way" of his own, but a radical one, to reach them.

Sanders wants a full-throated re-embrace of government, a correction from Clinton's anti-government pose. The former president embraced harsh policies on crime and welfare in part to win back whites; Sanders calls for nothing of the kind. Clinton helped the poor and middle class through stealth government—a vast and beneficial expansion of the Earned Income Tax Credit, a new college tuition tax credit program that, in terms of its value in foregone government revenues, matched the G.I. bill. Sanders, on the other hand, places government at the center of a new American revival, in which Medicare for all and tuition-free college promote greater opportunity and less income inequality.

So while it would be wrong to belabor the comparability of the two men, we have to acknowledge we've wound up in much the same place, almost 30 years after Clinton and his allies began their reclamation project: trying to lure white non-college voters to a party that has increasingly become a home to women, people of color, LGBT voters and "cosmopolitans" of every stripe—only immeasurably more so, this time around.

This is my third roundtable. I have not given up our common project on finding ways to win more white working class votes. But in the age of Trump, which I hope will be a short one, I believe it's more difficult, and more politically treacherous. Democrats began to hemorrhage white working class voters when Lyndon Johnson put the party behind civil rights in 1964. Their share of those voters dropped from 55 percent to 35 percent between 1964 and 1972. We have not figured out a way to win back a significant number of them without white-centering political corner-cutting, a la Clinton, ever since. But today, doing so is not just morally wrong, but politically risky, given the party's majority-female-and-voters-of-color base.

I was honored to be included in the 2012 Roundtable after I wrote "What's the Matter with White People?: Why We Long For A Golden Age That Never Was." The book tracked how the white working class became unmoored from the Democrats in the 1960s, partly through the story of my Irish Catholic family. While I acknowledged racism as a major factor in that breakup, I also made the case that the Democrats abandoned their role as the working-class party around the same time, making it hard to tease out which mattered more. I thought that if Democrats made a better, clearer case that they were the party of workers and not Wall Street, they could win back at least some of the defectors.

But even as I was writing it, I was questioning my thesis, shaken by the white backlash to President Obama, in which race undeniably played a role. Yes, Obama was too easy on Wall Street. But his auto bailout, his stimulus and even Obamacare provided tangible help to this group that I was insisting would reward Democrats for providing tangible help. They did not. Obama's support among WWC voters dropped from 40 percent against John McCain, in the middle of the terrifying financial crisis of 2008, to 36 percent against Mitt Romney, who looked not like a coworker but "the guy who laid you off," as Mike Huckabee noted 2008, and who emerged as the granite face of Bain Capital in 2012. In an afterward to the paperback, I tried to show how those Obama programs helped him in the Midwest, which they did, some. But where early exit polls showed him running ahead with the white working class in Ohio, thanks largely to the auto restructuring, later data showed he lost that group there, though he won narrowly in Wisconsin and Michigan.

Then came the race between Donald Trump and Hillary Clinton. We all know what happened. Or at least, we know that Trump, unbelievably, beat Clinton. We differ wildly over why. Many on the left have argued, with Bernie Sanders, that it was because even more white working class voters left the Democrats over the party's failure to broadcast an economic message that lined up with their experience of downward mobility and despair. I use the word "broadcast" because the party's platform was in fact the most progressive, both economically and socially, in my lifetime. I cannot deny there is some truth in that "broadcast" failure; reporters who try can easily find voters who say they backed Obama but abandoned Clinton, and who explain it's because they missed her economic message.

Still, a large and respectable roster of post-election surveys has shown us that the most salient factors in determining who voted for Trump is their racial resentment, belief in white superiority and fear of their coming "minority" status in the U.S. Meanwhile, historian Rick Perlstein reminds us that Trump's "Make America Great Again" echoed the Ku Klux Klan of the early 20th century (in a wonderful piece in which he takes some of his own earlier books to task). Trump tapped into an old, dark vein in American politics, and while we are right to look at the economic anxiety that helped him rise, we must also look at the racism.

Five years later, I've concluded my book was too respectful, in a way, of the white "ethnic" backlash against civil rights in the '60s. Partly because it was about my family: I tried to be compassionate, and located much of the backlash in their reaction to the genuine chaos of the times, not just around race, but also around drugs, crime, divorce, the sometimes violent anti-war movement, and so on. That was technically accurate, but I think it downplayed the role of racial and ethnic resentment. There is a strong, enduring, always-possibly-violent hostility to the "other" in American politics, despite the fact that most of us, or our families, were, at one point in American history, "the other" ourselves. Trump tapped into that fear and rage in a way Republicans like McCain and Romney had played with— McCain picked Sarah "pallin' around with terrorists" Palin as his running mate, and Romney sought and welcomed Trump's endorsement, even though his racist "birther" nonsense was the only thing that had made the swindling mogul a force in GOP politics—but had never fully deployed.

I wanted the solution to be for Democrats to promote strong populist economic policies, to stop kowtowing too much to Wall Street and, yes, even to change our approach to "identity politics," to some extent. But watching the backlash to Obama, then Clinton, even among some Obama voters -- when presented with a real, white, nativist "choice" in the person of Donald Trump -- I have come to despair that such an appeal will make an enormous amount of difference. For much of 2016, I felt like I wrote a manifesto for the Sanders movement back in 2012, but disowned it by the time Sanders ran.

[https://www.thenation.com/article/fear-of-diversity-made-people-more-likely-to-vote-trump/]

Of course I know Democrats have to win back at least some of these voters—if not to win the White House again (where the "rising American electorate" is still rising), then certainly to win back the Senate and especially the House of Representatives, along with purple-state legislatures which have gone bright red, enabling congressional conservatives to back punitive policies against women and people of color, from harsh voter suppression to surreal restrictions on reproductive rights. But so much of our current debate over Democratic strategy seems to center those white working class voters over the Democrats' most loyal constituencies, starting with black women (who gave Clinton 94 percent of their votes.)

Even Sanders, whose racial pitch grew more substantive and compassionate throughout the primary season, reverted to this tin-eared clunker in March: "I don't believe the majority of Trump voters are racist or sexist." We can't know whether he's right; he may be. We do know that some women and voters of color took his comment as a form of gaslighting: a denial of the very real racism and sexism that Trump deliberately channeled. Yes, Trump won even a majority of white women, and even some (we have no idea how many) white voters who backed Obama. But that doesn't erase Trump's victory's creepy undertones in white supremacy and misogyny.

We erase the acknowledgement of the primacy of racism at great political risk. Few people seem to remember it, but while Bill Clinton's racial signaling memorably won him back some white working class voters, in both the north and the south, it also seems to have cost him black votes. Where Walter Mondale and Michael Dukakis won 89 and 88 percent of the black vote in the 1984 and 1988 elections, according to the Joint Center for Political Studies, Clinton's support dipped to 82 percent in '92 and 84 percent in '96. Al Gore grabbed 90 percent running against George W. Bush four years later. Even accounting for the third party candidacy of Ross Perot (who won single-digit black support both years), Clinton suffered a noteworthy decline.

I admit that while writing my book, and after finishing it, I was chagrined by pushback from black friends and readers who believed I was minimizing the role of racism in the anti-Obama movement, as well as the difficulty of luring white working class voters without turning away the Democratic Party's loyal base of women and people of color. It's a painful admission, but I came to agree with them, especially as the Trump movement emerged. We are not here to relitigate the 2016 primary or general election; any fair observer must admit the problems with the Clinton campaign, including (especially?) the lack of a finely honed, fiery as well as compassionate economic message to those left behind in this winner-take-all economy. And yet any fair observer must also admit that when offered a message that reverberated with white nationalism, full of empty and contradictory and mostly unachievable economic policy proposals, a disturbing majority of white voters, particularly those we term "working class," signed on. And it's very hard to separate whiteness from the more understandable "nationalism" of Trump's white nationalist appeal.

There still remain opportunities to win some, maybe many, of those voters back. But now those chances mainly rest in the likelihood that Trump will betray them, as he is already doing. The man who promised to drain the political and economic "swamp" instead appointed swamp creatures to his cabinet. The guy who brayed against bankers and Wall Street and hedge funds appears to have delegated his appointments to the gang at Goldman Sachs, given how many company veterans have been placed in his executive offices. The Ryan-Trump Obamacare replacement could not have been designed to hurt Trump's voting base more if they'd set out to do so. The same goes for his proposed budget, which will devastate rural red states and counties.

Democrats must run on policies that center the working class—of every race. If they do, and if Trump fails as predicted, we will see a return of working class whites to the Democratic fold, perhaps even beyond the modest hopes—can we just climb back to Obama levels?—of many participants in this roundtable. But we can't advance those policies with denialist rhetoric that minimizes the role of racism in electing Trump and alienates the party's most loyal voters.

CAN THE DEMOCRATIC PARTY BE WHITE WORKING CLASS TOO?

Justin Gest

HELENA, MONTANA—Nothing about Steve Bullock bears a resemblance to Donald Trump. The son of educators, he had a humble, unremarkable upbringing in the Rocky Mountain town of Helena, Montana's state capital. He is less than comfortable in front of flashbulbs. A Columbia-trained attorney, he is happiest being left alone to study his briefing notes or the minutiae of legislation in his quiet office. His interactions with constituents come across as somehow unnatural but, humble and solicitous, his earnestness shines through anyway. The Democrat opened his first State of the State address in 2013 by saying, "My name is Steve and I work for the state." He is cautious about interviews with the press—not because he distrusts reporters, but because he wants to ensure he is fully prepared for any question that may arise. So when I interviewed him in the Governor's capital chamber, my first questio must have been some kind of nightmare.

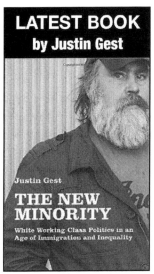

LATEST BOOK by Justin Gest

Justin Gest

THE NEW MINORITY

White Working Class Politics in an Age of Immigration and Inequality

Also by Justin Gest

Why Democrats lost the Rust Belt

Justin Gest's extensive field research among Rust Belt white working class Americans, presented in his book, The New Minority, reveals a complex range of attitudes beyond those captured by opinion polls. In a Vox interview, Gest discusses the unique insights his field research provides, insights that help explain white workers attitudes and political choices and why the Democrats lost their traditional support among these Americans.

http://www.vox.com/conversations/2016/12/21/14023688/donald-trump-white-working-class-republican-democrats-justin-gest

Justin Gest is the Author of The New Minority: White Working Class Politics in an age of Immigration and Inequality

"What do you and Donald Trump have in common?" I asked.

Shifting in his seat, he began to shuffle through the pages of prearranged notes sitting tidily on his lap. Finding nothing especially pertinent, he peered out a window, seeking a diplomatic but satisfying response from an unseasonably warm February afternoon. None came to mind.

"I've never spent time with Donald Trump, and I don't govern the same way," he finally said. Quizzically, the second-term Democrat added, "20 percent of my voters supported him on the same ballot though."

"Well that's just it," I said. "Surely, they must see something they like in both of you."

He reverted to his notes. "I think Montanans knew that I was fighting for them. I spoke about public education, public lands, public money, and those are things that affect us all. We hunt, we fish, and I asked whether we are promoting all Montanans' interests or only narrow special interests, and how we are going to build folks up individually."

85% White & Below Median Income

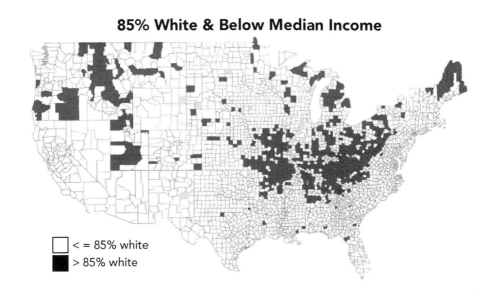

□ < = 85% white
■ > 85% white

85% White & Below Median Income

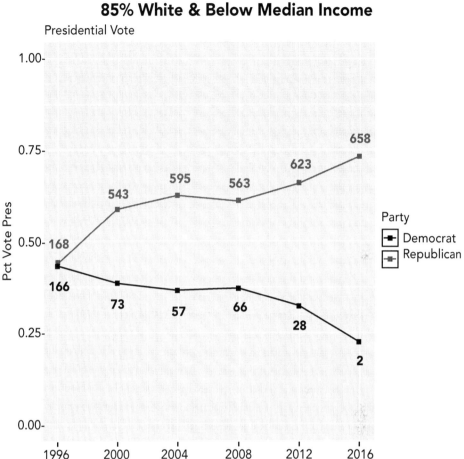

Figures indicate counties that are 85% or more white and below the national median income today and extrapolate backwards into the past to see how candidates perform in those same counties. By Justin Gest and Tyler Reny.

Perhaps realizing that this doesn't exactly coincide with most people's impression of the President, he added, "If there is overlap, it's making people know that I will fight for them, and that I work for them. I'm not sure that the values are that different in Manhattan, Montana; Manhattan, Kansas; or Manhattan, New York. People want to feel safe, have good schools, and want their kids to do better than they did."

Bullock's party colleagues in Washington are in a desperate search for ways they can appeal to those multiple Manhattans, but particularly to white working class people—a label that could apply to nearly all of Montana, and a constituency that Donald Trump and Republicans dominated to flip swing states and salvage contested House and Senate seats in the 2016 election.

The Democratic presidential candidate has won steadily fewer US counties with average incomes under the national median and with populations that are more than 85 percent white in every general election since 1996.

Concentrated in the Midwest, Appalachia and the Upper Rocky Mountains, there are 660 such counties today. Hillary Clinton won 2 of them.

What does Steve Bullock know that Hillary Clinton's army of consultants and advisors missed? Indeed, how can local politics inform a more national strategy for general elections and down-ballot races? In a predominantly white, working class state, Democrats have won four straight gubernatorial races, maintained one US Senate seat since 1913, and recently won a series of other statewide races until losing incumbents at Secretary of State and Attorney General last autumn. Do Montana Democrats have a template that can be applied elsewhere?

Great Falls is a gritty, working class town on the banks of the Missouri River, a hundred miles north of Helena. Its story is one heard in post-traumatic cities across the United States and Western Europe. An industrial hub that was once oriented around an Anaconda Company refinery, Great Falls understands loss.

Once America's fourth largest corporation with railroad, logging, mining and refining operations across Montana, Anaconda at one time provided a third of the state's paychecks. For nearly a century, its towering smoke-stack defined the city's northern skyline and stood as a 506-foot monument to Great Falls' industrial history, even after its associated factory was shuttered for 10 years. After "The Stack" was deemed to be structurally unsound in 1982, it was demolished in front of 40,000 witnesses—who watched as if it were the execution of a martyr. When the carefully set dynamite failed to collapse the hulking cylinder, leaving a stubborn shard of brick and mortar, onlookers rejoiced in triumphant defiance.

However, Great Falls has not been able to resist global trends. Its manufacturing sector has shrunk, unions were undercut, the surrounding landscape of ranchers now supplies an international market for meat and grain, and a once reliably Democratic region is far more contested by Republicans and frustrated by the status quo. Donald Trump voters who also supported Governor Steve Bullock abound.

In interviews with locals, I found exhaustion with detached national Democrats, and a pervasive appreciation of straight-talk.

Tom Conners has run the Steinhaus, a dive bar on Central Avenue, for 39 years. For four general election cycles, the 69-year-old has supported the Republican presidential candidate and a Democrat for Governor.

"One thing's for sure," he said from his perch on a barstool. "Trump'll have people out of the nest, all those politicians who are out for themselves and not for the country. I'm for the independent guy who doesn't bend over for this guy and that guy. I want to focus on this country. You can't solve the world's problems. And I think white working class people have a better chance with him. He has surrounded himself with people who are smarter than him. And they're people who know how to balance a budget and get things done like a business. I don't care about the wall, but I do care about infrastructure and focusing on this country. The reason why Donald Trump got elected is because the general working guy is infuriated by what's happened in Washington."

"But Bullock is different?" I asked, as Conners fed his customers' parking meters out front.

"Bullock isn't wishy-washy. Yeah, he's vetoed a few things since he's been in there, but he understands that you've got to take care of the dough. I was in debt once, but I made it work. You just don't buy your pet cup of coffee for a while. He gets that."

Amanda Sanne is a 25-year-old front desk manager at a roadside hotel. She and her husband both cast Trump-Bullock ballots last November.

"Donald Trump tried to make sure that you knew that your hard earned tax dollars were going to go to Americans," she said while shopping at a sporting goods store. "There are so many people living on assistance, and so much money goes out of the country. I just want a living wage and my rights. Hillary Clinton was very snobbish. She wanted to show that she's strong, but she was trying too hard to reach women and Mexicans. I think that sends a big message that she's more interested in their votes than those of the actual American people."

Lynn Berryhill is a 64-year-old interior designer and registered Democrat who voted for Bullock but could not bring herself to support Hillary Clinton. She voted for Gary Johnson instead.

"None of them know what it's like to scrounge, what normal people go through, living paycheck to paycheck, working day and night without having someone home to take care of the kids. So they lost the support of people who need the help. Politics is turning into high school gossip, and I'm giving up."

Dan Mathis is a 30-year-old nutrition retail salesman. Burly and blunt, he is an active homesteader, a Western tradition of settling wilderness for subsistence living. He voted for Donald Trump.

"There's just too much of a gap between my life and what Hillary Clinton does," he explained from the electrical aisle of a Great Falls farm store. "It is so isolated here. Most people never leave. So it's very hard to relate for the average person."

However, Mathis is deeply loyal to Bullock. He called the Governor's office when Montana's child protection agency dillydallied his partner's application for custody of his stepdaughter. Bullock's staff responded immediately.

"I thought I would leave a message and hear back in six months, but it was like that distance wasn't even there. It was almost personal, the way he was able to do that. At the time, I felt like I had no voice. Those little girls mean the world to me," he said, tearing up. "So I would go to the end of the earth for the Governor."

What makes Governor Bullock such an interesting case study for the Democratic Party is that he isn't exactly a unicorn—that rare, transcendent candidate whose personality crosses social divides.

Contrastingly, Bullock was preceded by the charismatic and bombastic Brian Schweitzer, a Democrat whose plain-spoken swagger appealed to Montanans and frustrated his rivals. Schweitzer famously wielded branding irons to publicly veto bills passed by a Republican-controlled legislature.

"I do best at explaining things by telling a story," Schweitzer told me by phone from Arizona. "Young people approach me who want to go into politics, and they ask me what to do. I would change your major out of political science or law. Get a practical trade, study science or math. Go out and try to change the world in the private sector. Start a business and lose it. Start a family. ...Do not learn how to run this country by working for people who already do. Look at Congressional staffers. In 20 years, they'll all be in office themselves—looking, talking, and droning on like the ones we have right now."

Schweitzer wasn't referring to Bullock, but the Governor could be forgiven for thinking so. Were he in Washington DC, Bullock would fit right in. Though gregarious, he is also cerebral, measured, even wonkish. After law school, he worked as a legal counsel to the Montana Secretary of State, and was later promoted to Executive Assistant Attorney General and Chief Deputy Attorney General before being elected Montana's Attorney General in 2008.

I asked Bullock if Schweitzer, whose name has been mentioned in 2020 presidential chatter, offered any memorable pieces of guidance before he was term-limited in 2012. "We lead in different ways," he said.

However, it is Bullock's way that Democrats are more capable of reproducing elsewhere. Without being that once-in-a-generation politician, he is able to connect with rural and working class white voters with symbolic messaging and a customized platform.

While I was in Great Falls, Bullock came to the A.T. Klemens metal shop to promote a new bill that would give tax credits to businesses that hired apprentices and veterans. He would later tour the workshop machinery and observe the craft of several young apprentices. It was all a bit forced, but what Bullock lacked in magnetism, he compensated for with his propensity to honor the past before pursuing the future.

"Hey, college isn't for everyone," a workshop supervisor told Bullock in a brief exchange. "It's a good living here, and you don't have loans to pay back. Sheet metalwork is a lost art. There's a shortage of labor supply in the trades. The kids just want electronics and college these days. They don't want to use their hands and work."

While many Democrats would roll their eyes, Bullock engaged him. "We look on the horizon and we think that's what's going to limit our growth is a shortage of guys like this. But that extends to other sectors like IT too."

This is novel. White working class people are accustomed to being considered anachronisms with no place in America's high-tech, information economy, foot-draggers slowing our evolution into a new economic and social era. In the 2016 election, Donald Trump was the first presidential candidate in a generation to make a deliberate appeal to this constituency and envision an economy that valued their contribution. Hillary Clinton was the establishment candidate, but also one who heralded and symbolized a future that reoriented the country's workplace, society, and relationship with a globalized world. The election was a referendum on America's past.

Based on a nationally representative poll of white Americans just before the 2016 primaries, new research shows that voters most attracted to Donald Trump and the far right perceive the greatest discrepancy between their status in today's society and the status of people like them 30 years before. Their sense of deprivation is nostalgic.

"Steve's been able to honor industries of the past," said Nancy Keenan, a past president of NARAL who now leads the Montana Democratic Party. "Timber, mining, coal. He has said that's part of who we are, but also talk about how do we grow and what the future looks like. He has been able to keep a foot in each of those worlds.

"He just recognizes economically a changing world. The days of mining—I grew up in a mining town, it's all we knew—you'll still have them as part of Montana's economy but it'll change because of technology and a global marketplace. It's goes back to trust. They trust him, and trust that he has their best interests at heart."

In Bullock's internal 2016 election polling, respondents reportedly shared largely favorable impressions of the Governor, but tend not to be able to point to a specific policy issue that he championed for them. He is likeable, and in many cases, that is enough.

Keenan insisted that her candidates can't win statewide office in Montana without a story. What is Steve Bullock's?

"I think Steve does connect with white working class voters," she said. "With his knowledge of Montana. He grew up here. He hunts and he fishes."

I asked the same question to Dave Hunter, a Montana political strategist since 1978. "White working class men like to hunt, and they like to fish," he said. "Fifty percent of Montana residents have a fishing license; twenty percent have a hunting license, and Bullock does too."

Even Andrew Bardwell, a 40-year-old bison rancher who I met in a farm store, said, "Bullock represents average Montanans. He hunts, he fishes, he's a businessman."

If it isn't abundantly clear, Bullock is from Montana. He likes to hunt. And he likes to fish.

"The irony is that I don't think he does," Hunter confessed. "Yeah he's hunted, but not for awhile. But it is the cultural messaging."

"Otherwise you don't pass the sniff test?" I asked.

"Yep. I mean, he can produce pictures of him and his buddies hunting. They put them up on Facebook, but I haven't seen one for 4 years. There's both a cultural test that is ethnocentric, and then you need an economic message. If you really are one of us, then people will listen to the economic message. If you're not really one of us, then nothing else matters."

Bullock's campaign exploited this ethnocentrism by drawing attention to his 2016 Republican opponent, businessman Greg Gianforte's roots in New Jersey and California. Gianforte might as well have been from Syria.

Every successful statewide Montana Democrat has been able to sell himself as an average, local man—and they all have been local men—even when there is countervailing evidence about how average they are. Not only do they revere the region's heritage; they embed themselves in it.

Montana's former at-large congressman, Pat Williams, served in the House of Representatives for 18 years and consistently made references to his jobs as a miner, sewer serviceman, and track layer for the Butte-Anaconda-Pacific railroad that hauled ore to smelters. Never mind that he held all those jobs before he graduated from college.

Longtime US Senator Max Baucus came from one of Montana's wealthiest families, but is known as a rancher from north of Helena who once walked 800 miles across Montana while campaigning.

Current Senator John Tester actively farms 1800 acres northeast of Great Falls and is prone to poking fun at city folk.

"It's authenticity," Keenan said. "Candidates have to be true to themselves. People want you be authentic, to share their experiences. When grain prices fall through the floor and the entire community is feeling the pinch, Montanans want you to understand that. You don't have to always agree with them, but you do need to look them into the eye and be honest with them. John Tester says, 'Don't tell me something's not happening with the climate; my crops are harvesting three weeks ahead.' His hands are in the dirt."

"The Democratic Party is full of these damned do-gooders," Keenan carried on. "A lot of the people who run as Democrats think that if we could just get into the depths and detail of the policy and make people understand it, then we'll get elected. Oh Hell no! The detail doesn't matter, people! What's the first rule of politics? Show up. Everywhere. The second rule is: Show up where they didn't want or ask you to come. I used to show up at the stock growers convention or the Chamber of Commerce conventions, and they'd all ask, 'What the Hell is she doing here?'" She guffawed. "And I'd tell everyone how terrific it was to be with them."

In an eerie echo, when I asked Governor Bullock what national Democrats need to do, he said, "They need to recognize that there are no such things as national issues; they're all local. It's not about pigeon-holing issues to score votes. Rule number one is to show up, and if you're just going to write-off parts of the country, your success will be limited. I think that we need to have a 50-state strategy. In 2008, you'd be tripping over Obama people [in Montana]. President Obama brought his wife and kids to the Butte 4th of July Parade. They lost Montana by 2 points, and he came after the primary."

Sitting inside Electric City Coffee in Great Falls, I listened to a conversation between old friends, Ken—a retired state transportation worker who is a Democratic-leaning independent—and Pat—a recently retired Army warehouse chief who voted for Bullock and wrote-in 'Justin Trudeau' rather than support Hillary Clinton.

"This isn't the party or the state I grew up with," Pat lamented. "We don't have two railroads, the unions are all but dead, the things that I remember in my formative years no longer exist. I think back to my sophomore year of high school, and Max Baucus came to our basketball game."

"Believe it or not, he came to work with us one day," Ken recalled. "We were painting stripes for the day, and we got him a hard hat and vest. That was in character with the guy. It showed he cares. You got any questions, he was there."

In an era when so much of politics is mediated by cable news, scripted social media missives, and airbrushed web profiles, showing up reveals candidates' humanity. It is where bonds are born.

But can stories laced with American nostalgia create bonds in coastal communities acutely aware of history's social ills, in economic power-houses forging a digital future? What bonds can emerge when the candidate who shows up is a shotgun-toting, coal-dusted, grain-farming moderate? Perhaps the Democratic Party is simply too unwieldy a coalition.

The January 21 post-inaugural protests revealed a leftist coalition comprised of everything from dreadlocks to Drybar, people part of labor unions and civil unions, arriving via transit but also Teslas. Can such an eclectic community expand to include the voices of marginalized white working class people from post-industrial spaces?

"You can't," Dave Hunter said. "There is a disconnect between the things a Democratic candidate has to do to win primaries in California and New York, and what is culturally acceptable for white persuadable voters in Montana. Look at Tester and Baucus, they are always running away from the national party. They pitch themselves as an independent voice for Montana. There isn't any national messaging. Running on a national party platform is death. In a state that is almost exclusively white, the imagery of the national Democratic Party as a multicultural, liberal, gun control, anti-coal party is tough messaging."

"How does someone like Steve Bullock win in Los Angeles, New York or Boston?" I asked.

"The flip side is that a candidate from one of those places with those views is going to have a rough ride in Montana," Hunter retorted.

"In Montana, yes, there is very little racial diversity, aside from Native Americans [who comprise about 6% of the state's population]," Keenan said. "But the other part is that folks never leave their county. They never go to a city. They might go to Billings, but I'd love to know the statistics about how many go to New York, DC, or Atlanta, because that's how you see what the rest of this country looks like. Republicans are much more homogenous."

That same homogeneity benefits Democrats in Montana. For example, whereas Georgia Democrats must bond with Atlanta's cosmopolitans and African Americans before rural white voters down the I-75 corridor, Montana Democrats' focus is undivided.

"Yeah, I suppose it's a benefit, the homogeneity," Bullock told me, upon reflection. "But if the premise is that Democrats have lost white working class men, then that could be a [national] problem, yeah. In 2020, you could weave together a coalition based on identity politics. If that's the bedrock foundation, you might win the presidency, but you'll lose the country. I don't want to be part of a party that ideologically only reflects the East and West Coasts. And while our experiences are different, I think a Native American, Latino, or me, as parents, have the same aspirations for our kids. Your hopes are the same."

However, many Democrats believe that broadening their party further only thins the ideological glue that holds them together. The more divergent, even deplorable, perspectives you integrate, the less you can meaningfully stand for, so the theory goes.

Currently, searching for rural Democrats in the national party caucus is, as they say in Montana, diggin' where there ain't no taters. There is space for Pat Williams who was broadly against gun control, Brian Schweitzer who supported the construction of oil pipelines, John Tester who pushed for the once-endangered grey wolf to be fair game. In turn, the party of diversity appears quite exclusive and inhospitable for key electoral constituencies.

Democrats must compromise or risk being ideologically "pure" but confined to their strongholds in coastal cities.

It is this supposed ideological purity that constitutes Democrats' greatest misperception.

The greatest ideological compromise likely came with the creation of the Democratic Leadership Council and the party's profitable alignment with the financial class, beginning in the late 1980s. Both a realization about the power of globalization and a reality of American campaign financing, Democrats' cultivation of liberal, urban cosmopolitans and professionals complicated their relationship with unions and working people who supported far more protectionist positions. And as Democrats have further embraced free trade, immigration, and cozied up to multinational corporations, white working class people who are not immigrants find less and less to like.

"Step by step, Democrats tried to broaden their base at the expense of working class families," said Leo Girard, the President of the Steelworkers Union. "You didn't lose the [2016] election because you had a shortage of rich white voters; you lost because working class people, unionists, had nowhere to go."

I refer to many of these white working class people as the Exasperated:

They feel betrayed by the countless politicians who have stood in front of shuttered mills and smelters and promised to bring manufacturing and mining economies back to life. It's why their counties have swung from party to party, from year to year—often reacting to the failures of previous candidates to deliver and sitting elections out. They are not "Independent" so much as they are just constantly disappointed. The Exasperated voted against Clinton in 2016 because, as a longtime member of the Washington establishment, she portended more broken promises. They voted for Trump because he was the first politician in a generation to make a deliberate, authentic pitch for their support.

What is so frustrating to older leftists is that Donald Trump resurrected the David versus Goliath themes that once characterized the older Democratic identity. Certainly, Democrats still support the wage standards, infrastructure, and redistributive policy prescriptions they once touted and have since been adopted by the President-elect.

Why can't these principles appeal to working class people—regardless of whether they are white?

I posed this question to Celinda Lake, Brad Martin, and Joe Lamson, strategists that have worked extensively in Montana. The consensus is that progressive platforms cannot be proposed without the cultural symbolism that "shows" rather than "tells" the white working class that they matter, that they belong.

"America is not a pretty place when things are contracting," said Lake, who runs a prominent polling firm in Washington DC. "Racism and sexism emerge when people think that America is losing its place—when things start to feel zero sum. And identity politics accentuates that. We articulated 'Stronger Together' with a divisive candidate and 'Together' didn't seem to include white, blue-collar types. They don't think they're part of that togetherness."

"In big races, Democrats would counsel people not to talk about religion," said Martin, who once oversaw the Montana Democratic Party and now runs its Oregon counterpart. "So Democrats, who were otherwise active members in their church, would do this weird dance around their faith. Same with guns. You're teaching Democrats to deny that they're a gun owner, rather than just say, 'Yeah I'm a gun owner, but I don't need an AK-47 to kill a deer.' All this took away the fact that Democrats were normal people. One pollster used to say that if your answers about gun control are 30 and 40 words long, you look like a teenager caught with a beer. You need to know the language of how people make their living, and stop comparing policy bullet points. You have to start talking about the things that affect their lives directly. Look at the signs for grocery stores around here: 'Beer. Ice. Ammo.' Well that says it right there."

To this point, Lake said that Trump voters were able to articulate the President's economic plan item-by-item in focus groups she conducted.

"Sure, they're working class economically, but it's more of a cultural difference now," said Lamson, who advised Pat Williams and Nancy Keenan's campaigns over the years. "What people don't like—regardless of whether you're in a reservation, a mill town, or a black community—is the politician just showing up out of nowhere to ask for votes. …I see bubbles all over, bubbles bumping into other bubbles. Trump supporters are in as much of a bubble or echo chamber as anyone else. [Democrats] just need to get out there and talk to people. Hillary's campaign could not fathom losing the Rust Belt, and they weren't speaking to their particular issues. Hillary's a good friend to the Williams in Montana, Chelsea spent time on ranches. But people just couldn't relate to her because they thought that she would take away their guns and shut down the natural resource industry. It was hard to go anywhere after that. …I mean, why are we spending all of our time talking about bathrooms? It's not that it's not important; it's just a matter of perspective."

Lake recalled a line Brian Schweitzer liked to use: 'Yeah I'm for gay marriage rights, but I think you care a whole lot more about whether there's grain on the High Line.'"

Donald Trump is not from Montana. He does not like to hunt. He does not like to fish.

The fact is that Montana has consistently voted for the Republican presidential candidate for decades and Hillary Clinton did not offer an appealing alternative.

But that a New York City aristocrat is recognized as the national voice of white working class people reveals how exasperated his supporters truly are, and how empty the field really is for candidates who want to compete with him for white working class support.

Many of his supporters in Montana remain wary.

Shane McCune is a 27-year-old tanner apprentice who spoke with Governor Bullock during his visit to the metal shop. "What do Democrats need to do to win white working class votes?" I asked him.

"Get us good jobs," he replied immediately. "Plain and simple. Seems like I got to work my butt off, and I barely get by. And then I see people on benefits having it so good. Stop giving them handouts. Around job sites, that's what people talk about. [Democrats] just need to get together, come up with some ideas, and follow through with them. It's a lot of little ideas. I don't know if Trump can do it."

"What if Trump fails to deliver?" I prodded.

"Then it's just another president. If there had been a better opponent, I may not have voted for Trump in the first place."

Shane's responses reveal both the contingency of his support for Donald Trump, but also the persistent dilemma for Democrats—showing that not only is there no tension between white working class people and other disadvantaged groups, but that their fates are actually linked.

Andrew Bardwell, the bison rancher, articulates this linked fate. He and his wife, Annie, met at a hunting camp and work as farm hands in Choteau, 50 miles northwest of Great Falls. Both are registered Democrats, Bullock voters, but were dissatisfied by Hillary Clinton's candidacy.

"I can't think of a single [trucking] rig with a Trump sticker on it, and I think most people don't think that Donald Trump is doing people like us any favors," he said. "None of his jobs are coming here. He wasn't talking about building elevators on the High Line. We export everything we produce—our wheat, our barley, our children—so his anti-trade thing is going to kill us. I just think that people around here are scared shitless about Hillary Clinton taking their guns away. And I know that sounds trite, but they are scared shitless. She connected with no one.

"A lot of the time, there is an impression that Republicans represent independent, flag-waving Americans. But in a rural environment, we have to realize that we are highly dependent on public services. The kids are going to be the only ones on a school bus that takes them 25 miles to the nearest school. We use roads that are built into the countryside to serve just a few people.

"Many Trump voters are close friends and family of mine. And I think they fail to see the irony. You can't sit there and complain about freeloaders. They think they're doing God's work and feeding the people, but we overproduce and export most of our goods. And they don't realize how much the government does. Think of price supports on grain, which has an effect on the cost of beef. And so while Christianity and the second amendment are core values for us, it doesn't trump our other values."

Mere months ago, the conventional wisdom was that it was the Republican Party that was near implosion. Whether authors were referring to the Republican Party's electoral chances or its historic profile as a party of small government, fiscal responsibility, foreign engagement, and neoliberalism, the message was clear: Donald Trump has crafted a Republican Party that marginalizes the people who believed in these bedrock principles, and narrowed its focus to a hard core of bitter white people who yearn for yesteryear. Few anticipated the power of partisan ties, and Hillary Clinton could not poach moderate Republicans and Independents to the extent many expected.

What if moderate white voters would have turned out and voted Democratic had anyone other than Hillary Clinton been running? What if Trump disappoints a significant share of white working class voters?

Unless Democrats meaningfully reach out and connect with these groups, we will never know.

No doubt, much of the national partisan landscape depends on how Donald Trump and Congressional Republicans govern. But for Democrats, this is also a question of how inclusive their party really is.

Justin Gest is an Assistant Professor of Public Policy at George Mason University's Schar School of Policy and Government, and author of The New Minority: White Working Class Politics in an Age of Immigration and Inequality.

The following is a brief excerpt from Gest's book:

The New Minority: White Working Class Politics in an Age of Immigration and Inequality

The result of the difficulties encountered by mainstream American and British political parties is a vast sector of the electorate that has been uninspired, but also largely unsolicited, by political campaigns. White working class people in the American Rust Belt are conventionally thought of as a swing vote, because of their unpredictability and a lack of loyalty to either party at the national level. In both countries, great rewards await the party that finds a way to sustainably reintegrate them as part of a grander coalition. Republicans and Tories seek a new, expanded base of voters to compete with Democrats' and Labour's growing demographic edges. Democrats, in particular, could seal their national dominance by attracting a broader spectrum of working class voters. If any party chooses to make this appeal, there are a number of gaps that a future generation of leaders may fill:

Recruit candidates from the ranks of the non-elites. It is not sufficient to hammer the excesses of big business and cast the other side as the keepers of an elitist plutocracy. Working class voters want to see candidates with working class backgrounds. Democrats should not simply assume that their opposition will always be led by a private equity tycoon—a circumstance which made them look working class by comparison in 2012. In fact, the median net worth of Democratic Members of the House of Representatives has risen substantially, up nearly $200,000 in inflation-adjusted dollars just between 2004 and 2009 (Center for Responsive Politics 2013). Meanwhile, the median net worth of Republican House Members was down by nearly the same amount over that time period, closing the gap between the parties to less than $100,000 (ibid.). The white working class understands that politicians likely won't have calloused hands, but they also yearn to see their own reflection in a representative who understands manual labor. It's not enough to produce candidates who attempt to connect with the middle class based on their ancestry—for example by indicating that at some point in their family lineage; someone was middle or working class. The African-American, Latino, and lesbian and gay communities can all see visible representation in party leadership; the white working class wants no less.

Employ working class narratives. When candidates are not working class themselves, they can still show signs of empathy by channeling the language and lifestyle of constituents. That means making reference to their realities of unstable jobs, declining wages and benefits, and a greater strain on family life because of these burdens. It also means emphasizing the common goal that everyone should be able to work one job, forty hours a week, and take care of their families. Working class voters see the parties doing visible outreach to other constituent communities and they want the same consideration and thought put toward wooing them. They will listen for language that explicitly includes them and lifts them up, favoring politicians who try to earn their vote over those who simply assume they have it.

Do not conflate the working class with the helpless. Most working class people are not earning the minimum wage, nor do they think of them-selves as reliant on government welfare programs (even when they are benefiting from many of them). They want to be seen as independent, self-sufficient, and hard-working, and as such, they won't be satisfied by a candidate or party who simply promises to protect or expand poverty assistance programs or raise the minimum wage. They want to know that their political leaders both understand their struggles, and distinguish them from those of people who are another rung down on the income ladder.

Do not assume unions are synonymous with the working class. Times have changed, and most white working class people are not unionized anymore. Both parties and candidates must eschew shortcuts, address their constituents directly, and stop simply depending on unions as interlocutors— especially given that unions' status with many of these voters is questionable at best, as this book shows.

Challenge nostalgia with hope. This book has demonstrated the mobilizing power of nostalgia but also its destructive consequences. No party will ever deliver on promises to turn back the clock, so leaders must seize the challenge to envision a future that incorporates white working class people into the global economy and into coexistence with ethnic minorities. There is an opportunity waiting for leftist leaders who can appeal to white working das voters in these ways, especially if they go hand in hand with pursuing labor standards and strengthening social protections.

Ultimately, contrary to conventional portrayals, white working class voters are rational. The seek representatives who care about their grievances. They seek platforms that act on these grievances. And they respond to parties and organizations that invest in them with time, resources, and candidates. This is not different from any other sector of the electorate. The difference is that social and economic forces have isolated the white working class as a political constituency, to the extent that many in this demographic feel like a peripheral afterthought in a country they once defined. A group with a powerful vote has thus been neglected, and populists are beginning to take notice.

A REVIEW OF TWO IMPORTANT SOCIOLOGICAL FIELD STUDIES OF WHITE WORKING AMERICANS: ARLIE HOCHSCHILD'S *STRANGERS IN THEIR OWN LAND* AND KATHERINE CRAMER'S *THE POLITICS OF RESENTMENT.*

Robert Kuttner

The following excerpts are from American Prospect editor Robert Kuttner's December 2016 review article on the white working class that illustrate the unique insights ethnographic field studies can contribute to Democratic political strategy.

"Five years ago, the sociologist Arlie Hochschild set out to better understand what she called the "deep story" of the mostly white, mostly downwardly mobile Americans who made up the fervent constituency of the Tea Party, and now of Donald Trump. These are the people who ostensibly vote against their economic self-interests, as Thomas Frank contended more than a decade ago in *What's the Matter with Kansas?* They loathe a government that often redistributes and regulates in their favor.

Also by Robert Kuttner:

The discussion of Arlie Hochschild and Katherine Cramer's field studies presented here are taken from a more extensive review by American Prospect editor Robert Kuttner that is titled:

Hidden Injuries of Class, Race and Culture: The Decline of the White Working Class and the Rise of The Tea Party and Donald Trump

The review includes discussion of books by John Judis, Thomas Frank and J.D. Vance and several others as well as of Hochschild and Cramer.

http://prospect.org/article/hidden-injuries-0

Robert Kuttner is an Editor of The American Prospect

What was at work here?, Hochschild wanted to know. What was their "narrative as felt"? Her odyssey took her to an ideal locale to fathom the apparent cognitive dissonance of the right-wing populist backlash—the swampy region around Lake Charles, Louisiana, a town of 75,000 all but ruined by the petrochemical industry.

In ten extended trips to southwest Louisiana, Hochschild proceeded with great humility, sitting around kitchen tables, taking drives, going to church, listening respectfully to the life stories of 60 people, accumulating 4,690 pages of transcript. Despite their political differences, she grew to like, even admire, most of them, for their generosity and fortitude.

Hochschild's account, *Strangers in Their Own Land*, is novelistic as well as an exemplary political ethnography. Her tale is at once baffling, demoralizing, and a wake-up call for liberals. It is the clearest narrative exposition yet of the social basis of the Trump backlash and of right-wing populism generally.

"Virtually every Tea Party advocate I interviewed for this book," she writes, "has personally benefited from a government service or has close family who have. Several have elderly disabled parents and had them declared indigent in order to enable them to receive Medicaid." Louisiana, like most red states, is a net recipient of federal aid; the lower you go on the income ladder, the more pronounced is that cost-benefit tilt in your favor.

Places like southwest Louisiana also desperately need government protection from predatory industry. A region that these adults remember as a paradise of plentiful fishing, hunting, swimming, and boating on lovely bayous is now a substantially uninhabitable landscape, due to the predations of companies like Union Carbide and PPG. Water cannot be safely drunk and is dangerous to swim in. The fish are mostly gone or toxic to eat. Methane seeps out of the earth. Birds are dying. Nearby, along the Mississippi River, is an 85-mile strip of more than 150 chemical plants, widely known as Cancer Alley because of the elevated cancer rates linked to toxic waste. One of Hochschild's interviewees, Mike Schaff, lost his home and neighborhood to a giant, 30-plus-acre sinkhole in Bayou Corne that was created when salt domes rented for toxic storage by chemical companies gave way. The locals are indeed strangers in their own land.

Hochschild writes, "I feel as if I've come upon the scene of a slow-motion crime."

Touring the lost world of a 77-year-old Cajun man named Harold Areno, in Bayou d'Inde, Hochschild is introduced to scenes of dead cypress trees, blind turtles, and species of fish and game that either no longer exist or are toxic. As she grasps the personal impact and environmental catastrophe caused by insufficiently policed chemical dumping, Hochschild writes, "I feel as if I've come upon the scene of a slow-motion crime."

Yet to a person, her interviewees hate the Environmental Protection Agency, and vote for political leaders who want to shut it down. Even Mike Schaff, who personally crusaded against the chemical companies at risk to his own livelihood, votes Tea Party.

How can this possibly be? These people, after all, are not stupid. More to the point, she finds, they are good, worthy, likable folk, quick to help a neighbor in distress. To summarize a complex human story that deserves to be read in all its rich detail, here's what she finds:

People hereabouts don't trust government, state or federal, and not without reason. They've watched, close-up, as the government of Louisiana, one of the most chronically corrupt, has given the oil and chemical industry a free pass. The federal EPA may be somewhat better, but it is even more remote, and seems to care more about protecting obscure species than saving bayous. But the government is great at extracting taxes, often to help people who don't deserve it, and at adding nuisance regulations. If the government had been doing its job, their homes would not have been turned into a ruined landscape of toxic waste. The most fervent recruits to the Tea Party, as Alec MacGillis has observed, are not working-class, much less underclass. They are dispossessed middle-class, who see neither political party respecting, much less serving, them. Government promised, didn't deliver, and tendered visible help mainly to the dependent poor. Genuine benefits like Social Security, Medicare, and Medicaid aren't enough to tilt the balance.

Hochschild's Louisiana friends derive their view of government not from what it might be but from what it is, in their own experience.

Unlike hopeful liberals, Hochschild's Louisiana friends derive their view of government not from what it might be but from what it is, in their own experience. Harold Areno puts it just about perfectly:

> The state always seems to come down on the little guy. Take this bayou. If your motorboat leaks a little gas into the water, the warden'll write you up. But if companies leak thousands of gallons of it and kill all the life here? The state lets them go. If you shoot an endangered brown pelican, they'll put you in jail. But if a company kills the brown pelican by poisoning the fish he eats? They let it go. I think they overregulate the bottom because it's harder to regulate the top.

This view sounds almost like something Bernie Sanders or Ralph Nader might say, but it leads to an opposite brand of populism—a sense of both resignation and deep resentment, a feeling that all we can rely on is our own grit; even an acceptance of environmental destruction as the price that must be paid for jobs (though the jobs are becoming unreliable). Jackie Tabor, one of her subjects, tells Hochschild without a shred of irony, "Pollution is the sacrifice we make for capitalism."

That sensibility is what makes these folks right-wing populists. They hate all things big, including big business and big government, and they correctly see the two as conjoined. Based on their own lived experience, they have no confidence that government, as John Kenneth Galbraith hoped, can serve as a countervailing force against business for the benefit of the people. Culturally, Hochschild reports, they seek "relief from liberal notions of what they should feel—happy for the gay newlywed, sad for the plight of the Syrian refugee, un-resentful about paying taxes."

How do the good people of Lake Charles cope if they don't look to government for help? They have their church. Harold Areno, mourning his lost cypress trees, says thoughtfully, "They say there are beautiful trees in Heaven." And they have each other—their own sense of community decency and proud self-reliance. They are victims who reject a language of victimhood, Hochschild writes. Government seems not to respect any of this.

Hochschild puts her finger on something that has eluded many analysts who focus on the economics, namely the role of culture. These people feel condescended to. "They … felt culturally marginalized: their views about abortion, gay marriage, gender roles, race, guns, and the Confederate flag all were held up to ridicule in the national media as backward," she writes. "They felt like a besieged minority." One of her interlocutors tells her, "[T]here are fewer and fewer white Christians like us."

After considering her interviews at length, Hochschild synthesizes what she takes to be the credo of the Tea Party supporters of southwest Louisiana:

You see people cutting in line ahead of you! … Through affirmative action plans, pushed by the federal government, they are being given preference for places in colleges and universities, apprenticeships, jobs, welfare payments, and free lunches. … Women, immigrants, refugees, public sector workers—where will it end? Your money is running through a liberal sympathy sieve you don't control or agree with. …

Unbelievably, standing in front of you in line is a brown pelican.

The credo is not just about economic displacement. It's about honor. The Tea Party supporters of Lake Charles are no longer honored, either as whites, or as male breadwinners, or as women homemakers.

Regional honor? Not that either. You are often disparaged for the place you call home…. There is a political movement of people such as yourself who share your deep story. It's called the Tea Party.

Hochschild emails her rendition of what she calls "The Deep Story" to the people who have become her Louisiana friends. One emails back, "I live your analogy." Another says, "You've read my mind."

Her subjects go out of their way to tiptoe around race, though it is tacitly present. There was a time when government delivered enough that people like them could feel that government was on their side. Their grandparents voted for Huey Long, and for FDR. Once, Louisiana regularly elected Democrats. For most of the 20th century, they enforced racial segregation. Now, government seems to be an alliance between the lowest classes, racial minorities, and the culturally avant-garde. The government not only insists on race-mixing but expects welcoming smiles.

IN *THE POLITICS OF Resentment*, political scientist Katherine J. Cramer conducts hundreds of interviews with residents of rural Wisconsin, seeking to learn why the state that elected Robert La Follette, William Proxmire, and Russ Feingold has Scott Walker as its governor. She finds "people making sense of politics in a way that places resentment towards other citizens at its center." In particular, rural Wisconsinites in the northern part of the state, most of whom have lost income and economic security in recent decades, feel that the big cities are taking too much at their expense.

The state's biggest city happens to be Milwaukee, a city with a large black population. The other large city, Madison, combines the ultra-liberalism of a Cambridge or a Berkeley with the role of state capital. Small-town Wisconsin increasingly abhors Madison for both reasons. As the rest of the economy has lost income and economic security, the public employees who once had a pay package that seemed merely normal now seem to be enjoying privileges financed by the tax dollars of people who are worse off. "The teachers union," says a man named Harold. "They were in there like the cat at the bowl of milk. Then they turned it to cream. Then they turned it to ice cream." Harold, it turns out, is a former member of the United Automobile Workers, a union that epitomizes the shrinking blue-collar economy.

Race and the perception of racial favoritism compound the problem. "They give everything to Milwaukee," says one of Cramer's subjects. The old liberal formula of tax, spend, and regulate has ceased to be effective or persuasive. Government itself is the enemy.

The comments quoted by Cramer could have been from Hochschild. The political sentiments that result seem Southern. But here they are, in one of the great progressive northern states. It's true that Wisconsin has a history of going right as well as going left. This was Joe McCarthy's state, too. And that's the point—populism can go either way, whether the driver is downward mobility, or nationalist anxiety over communists or Muslims. In Wisconsin, at this writing, Clinton is up just five points over Trump.

Many whites attracted to the populist backlash also feel beleaguered as Christians. As Robert P. Jones, a mainstream scholar of religion and columnist for *The Atlantic*, writes in *The End of White Christian America*, both mainline and evangelical Christian denominations consider themselves to be sadly in decline. The statistics, of which Jones provides plenty, bear that contention out. As a share of the population, self-described evangelicals have declined from 22 percent in 1988 to 18 percent in 2014. Mainline Protestants have dwindled more precipitously, from 24 percent to 14 percent.

The cherished community is the church. The state has no place.

You might think, with Schaller and Teixeira, that these trends would lead to a declining religious influence on politics. But the sense of an alien, secular society disrespecting traditional faith and values leads to intensified fervor, especially in the red states (and some swing states) where religious conservatives are concentrated. And another paradox: While support for some social issues such as same-sex marriage has grown among evangelicals, the effort to use religious teachings and values to enlist evangelicals to join a progressive pocketbook coalition has failed to materialize. PICO, a respected coalition of progressive faith-based groups, is heavily rooted in mainline Protestant, left-Catholic, and Jewish congregations. One reason, observes Richard Parker, who teaches religion and politics at Harvard's Kennedy School, is that evangelical teachings stress the direct connection between the congregant and the Lord. The cherished community is the church. The state has no place.

IN SUM, AMERICAN progressivism today is foundering on what we might call *the clash of deeply felt injuries.* The insecurity and downward mobility of the white working and middle classes collides with a well-justified upsurge in black consciousness of continuing racial outrages and a demand for their remediation. Feminists and oppressed cultural minorities pile on. Today's story is one of dueling cultural and economic wounds, each with substantial basis in reality.

It's hard to tell white hillbillies, residents of Lake Charles or of rural Wisconsin, to "check your privilege," when they are far less privileged than their parents or grandparents. It's liberal and conservative elites whose children are privileged. The charge of political correctness, used so deftly by Trump, resonates with white workaday voters in part because liberals seem to give priority to every other downtrodden group, from illegal aliens (sic) to transgender people to brown pelicans. The rainbow parade on display at the recent Democratic National Convention epitomizes everything workaday conservatives of the sort interviewed by Hochschild and Cramer hate about liberals.

WHITE WORKING CLASS VOTERS DIFFER NOT JUST IN "WHAT THEY THINK" BUT "HOW THEY THINK". UNDERSTANDING THIS DIFFERENCE IS THE KEY TO CREATING A SUCCESSFUL DEMOCRATIC STRATEGY

Andrew Levison

Looking at the details of the 2016 election, one can argue that any alternative strategy may have offered a plausible scenario for a Democratic victory. A different candidate, better advertising and voter targeting, better basic messaging and plat-form—changing any one of these factors can very convincingly be argued to have been sufficient to reverse the outcome.

But if one steps back and looks at the 2016 election in longer term perspective, the most important conclusion is that after 16 years and five presidential elections, Democrats have profoundly failed to expand the sociological base of their coalition. The geographic and demographic profile of Hillary Clinton's support in 2016 looks almost identical to the

LATEST BOOK
by Andrew Levison

THE
WHITE
WORKING
CLASS
TODAY

Who They Are,
How They Think
and How Progressives
Can Regain Their Support

ANDREW **LEVISON**

Also by Andrew Levison:

During the two years pre-ceding the 2016 election, Andrew Levison published several extremely prescient articles about the urgent need for Democrats to in-crease their support among white working class voters:

Why Democrats Still Need Working Class White Voters (with Ruy Teixeira)

https://newrepublic.com/article/113380/why-democrats-still-need-working-class-white-voters

Democrats Have a White Working Class Problem—and not just in the South

https://newrepublic.com/article/118960/democrats-white-working-class-problem-isnt-just-south

Andrew Levison is Co-Director of the White Working Class Round-table and author of The White Working Class Today

contours of Al Gore's support in 2000. The Democratic coalition remains based on almost exactly the same "McGovern coalition" of minorities, youth, single women and educated professionals that Ruy Teixeira and John Judis identified almost 15 years ago in their book, *The Emerging Democratic Majority*. Despite the very gradual demographic change that the book accurately projected, it is this limitation of the Democratic coalition that not only makes the Democratic candidate still very vulnerable during presidential elections but has allowed Republicans to hold stable control of the House of Representatives and dominate state-level politics across the country.

The most glaring weakness in the modern Democratic coalition is the decline of white working class support that once provided a major pillar of the Democratic Party. In 2008, even in the midst of a massive and terrifying economic crisis and an unprecedented military fiasco, Barack Obama still received only 40 percent of the white working class vote. In 2012 Obama's share declined to 36 percent and in this year's election, Hillary Clinton suffered an unprecedented 8 percent additional drop in white working class support according the the exit polls, her share of that vote declining to an abysmal 28 percent.

The general interpretation of Trump's gain among white working class voters has been that he won this additional 8 percent support over the basic 60-64 percent level of white working class support for the GOP in recent years by adding a combination of more explicit racism and ethno-nationalism, a direct appeal to a sense of economic distress and social abandonment, and a faux-populist, media savvy identification with working people.

The many first-hand journalistic accounts of white working class Trump supporters, particularly in the Rust Belt, have tended to be relatively sympathetic. While recognizing the substantial role played by Trump's appeal to bigotry, these accounts generally portrayed white working people as angry over economic decline, frustrated with their loss of their former status in society, and deeply resentful of the ill concealed distain of Democratic liberals.

On this basis, the Democratic debate has focused on two opposing proposals for Democratic strategy. The first views white workers' support for Trump as largely motivated by racism, a view that leads to the conclusion that Democrats should abandon the attempt to regain white working class votes and concentrate on raising the turnout of the existing Democratic coalition. The second proposal holds that white workers have legitimate issues and justifiable complaints about their economic circumstances and Democratic indifference. This leads to the belief that Democrats can regain the support of white working class voters without having to compromise the existing Democratic platform if Democrats will just offer a firmly progressive, full-throated version of economic populism.

There is, however, a fundamental problem with both these views and, indeed, this basic way of thinking.

Both of these approaches view the white working class as a relatively homogeneous social group—one whose members think about politics and make political choices and decisions in largely similar ways. In this conception white working class voters differ from each other essentially because they are arrayed along different points on a single political continuum, one that ranges from Conservative Republican to Progressive Democrat.

In reality, however, there are actually two fundamentally different kinds of white working class voters. They differ not just in *"what they think"* (their opinions on issues) but *"how they think"* (their way of making political choices and decisions). Understanding this difference is the indispensible key to creating a successful Democratic strategy.

There are obviously important demographic subgroups and polarities within the white working class: young versus old, men versus women and so on. But the existence of these demographic segments is actually not the decisive issue. In the practical political world of door to door canvassing for political candidates or in grass roots organizing campaigns, political strategy is always based on one fundamental three-way division of any target group—between those who are already on our side, those who are unalterably against us, and the ambivalent or persuadable group in the middle.

Here's a very typical chart used in Democratic political campaigns:

	Progressive / Democrat	Ambivalent / Persuadable	Conservative / Republican
Always Votes	In the bag	High priority Persuasion	ignore
Sometimes Votes	High priority turnout effort	High priority Persuasion	ignore
Never Votes	Low priority turnout effort	Low priority persuasion	ignore

Grass roots organizers who do door to door canvassing use the same basic framework. Here is Karen Nussbaum, president of Working America, describing the basic approach her organization employs:

> *Working America engages not the fixed 30-35 % or so at each end of the political spectrum (including the firm conservatives who are not and never will be with us on the issues) but rather the 30-40% in the middle. Working class moderates whose personal ambivalences make them swing voices in the public policy debates.*[1]

In the practical setting of particular campaigns the need to focus strategy on the persuadable sector of a target group is always recognized, but in broad discussions of strategy the critical distinction between persuadable and non-persuadable voters frequently gets lost. In discussions about the white working class, in particular, the objective frequently becomes defined as *"winning back the white working class"* in general rather than *"winning back the persuadable sector of the working class."* The first is an impractical objective that leads to impractical strategic ideas; the second is the basis for any successful political strategy.

Seen in this light the key questions then become, first, are these "persuadable" white working class voters basically similar to other more partisan pro-GOP white workers or are they in some way a cognitively and psychologically distinct group, and, second, what proportion of these persuadable voters can actually be convinced to vote for Democrats and what proportion will tend to express their ambivalence in other ways such as support for independent candidates or a refusal to vote at all.

Guess what: the conclusions you reach about the psychology of persuadable white working class voters depends on the methodology you use to study them.

Most discussions of Democratic strategy are based on opinion polls and these, by their nature, tend to focus on people's specific opinions about which candidate they favor or their views on particular political issues.

But both the Senatorial and presidential vote in 2016 showed that traditional polls failed to provide adequate guidance for political strategy. While national opinion polls did indeed accurately predict the presidential vote to within less than 2 percent, polls in key states substantially underestimated the likely strength of Trump's appeal to white working class voters on Election Day, leading to major errors in voter targeting and messaging. The newer techniques of "microtargeting" and "data mining" were also given glowing coverage in the press during the campaign. They were hailed as incredibly accurate ways to identify and communicate with voters down to the level of specific individuals—but the election results showed that their power and accuracy was vastly overhyped. Indeed, the results made clear that the major tools for understanding white working class Americans were simply not adequate.

In the spring of 2016 I had the opportunity to collaborate on the design and execution of a large, highly innovative focus group project that examined "persuadable" white workers in a more specific way and in greater depth then had previously been undertaken. The large battery of focus groups in this project were conducted by Guy Molyneux of Hart Research for The Fair Deal Project and Guy has summarized his conclusions from this research in an article in the winter issue of *The American Prospect*.[2]

There were two innovative aspects to the Hart Research/Fair Deal focus groups:

First, the participants were limited to a very carefully defined group of voters—individuals with less than a college education who were not firm or consistent Democrats or Republicans but were rather "independents" or very weak Democratic or Republican supporters. The participants were also limited to those who described themselves as either "middle of the road" or only "somewhat liberal" or "somewhat conservative."

(Although people with a "less than college" education work in a wide variety of jobs, a substantial portion of the occupations held by the men in these focus groups were very distinctly the kinds of jobs that most people do think of as traditionally "working class"—mechanic, heating and air technician, laborer, plumber, truck driver, parts manager, shift supervisor, contractor, automotive equipment salesman, carpenter.

Very few focus groups have ever focused this precisely on "ambivalent" or "persuadable," less than college educated white working class workers. The carefully narrowed focus makes a profound difference in the results that are obtained because a more typical focus group that also includes individuals with strong progressive or conservative opinions often tends to get shaped or even "hijacked" by the ideologues". Even participants who disagree with more extreme positions end up having to define their own opinions in reaction to the strong views that are expressed by others rather than being able to let their own perspective spontaneously emerge. In such situations, "middle of the road" participants never get to talk and share ideas with others similar to themselves.

The second important characteristic of these particular focus groups was simply their size. The project included eight different groups that included a total of 80 participants. This made it possible to create separate focus groups with standard, identical formats for specific demographic groups like young men, older men, young women and older women, and to also situate four of the groups in the north and another four in the south.

This was also a key step. Heterogeneous groups that include both men and women and a range of ages make it very hard to clearly distinguish the views of the various subgroups involved. Men do not speak the same way in groups with women as they do among themselves, while older men will often acknowledge thoughts and feelings among themselves that they do not express in front of younger people.

As a result, with this design it became possible to separately examine the views of persuadable white working class men and persuadable white working class women as well as different age and regional groups.

In this article, the views of white working class men will be examined.

The most important characteristic of these middle of the road white male workers is that they approach politics using a fundamentally distinct cognitive framework than do white workers who hold a firm conservative or progressive ideology. In Molyneux's *American Prospect* article he uses the term "white working class moderates"[3] as a succinct way to characterize these Americans—but it is worth noting that this is not how they generally would describe themselves. They themselves tend to describe their approach to making political decisions as using *"practical common sense,"* or *"my personal philosophy."* They see themselves as trying to *"think for myself"* to *"make up my own mind," "do my own thinking"* or *"see both sides"* of an issue. When analyzing a political topic they will often use a distinct *"one the one hand, on the other hand"* mode of thought.

This is a fundamentally different way of thinking about political issues than the method used by individuals who are firmly committed to an organized political ideology. It is not just a matter of *"what they think,"* it is a matter of *"how they think."* The many white working class followers of Rush Limbaugh or Sean Hannity or the latest conservative televangelist all very emphatically reject the idea of trying to *"see both sides"* of political issues. They believe very deeply that there are radically distinct "right" and "wrong" views on all political issues and that their particular views are firmly and entirely based on the former.

One consequence of this difference between the two ways of thinking was very apparent in the way the individuals in the male focus groups in the project related to each other. There was virtually no angry, dogmatic assertion of opinions or deprecation of other people's views—things that quite often occur in discussions in which ideologues participate. On the contrary, the individuals in these particular focus groups were entirely friendly and respectful to each other and frequently seemed pleased and stimulated by having the opportunity to share, exchange and compare ideas with people similar to themselves.

Observing the groups there were three significant patterns that emerged:

I. These white workers were overwhelmingly cultural traditionalists -- but their comments illustrated the fact that there is a fundamental difference between cultural traditionalism and conservatism.

Cultural traditionalism is often confused with conservatism because people who are ideological conservatives very often uphold and glorify traditional cultural ideas. But cultural traditionalism is a distinct concept from conservatism, one that refers to a set of basic social values that exist in working class life and not to specific social or political views. Within this set of basic traditional social values various perspectives can exist, perspectives that can range from firmly conservative to strongly progressive.

There are three major traditional values in white working class culture: respect for religious faith, respect for military service and respect for the character traits encouraged by small business, honest labor and hard work. Each of these traditional values is supported by community social institutions like the church, the military and the business community and is continually reinforced by family, friends and neighbors as a working person grows up in his or her community.

1. Working class and small business values

Unlike the industrial era when "working class values" were defined by industrial labor, today working class and small business values significantly overlap, especially among groups like worker-contractors in construction. Pride in craftsmanship, the character building value of hard work and self-discipline and similar traditional working class values are now intermixed with values related to small business, values like independence, individual initiative and pride in making a small business a success.

The focus group participants expressed a variety of views endorsing these values as ones they deeply held and wanted to transmit to their children. They complained about the fact that the modern "lousy jobs" economy undermined these values; that they could no longer find jobs where they experienced the pride that comes from being a craftsman, from doing "a hard day's work and earning a good living" or making long-term sacrifices that provided a better life for their family. They also bemoaned the fact that the modern economy has made it very difficult to teach their children the character-building nature of hard work -- the deep satisfaction of rebuilding a car engine or framing a garage addition by hand. They expressed classic attitudes about valuing the pride that comes from being a productive member of society. *"I don't want to just be given anything"* one said, *"I want to earn my living."*

Alongside these traditional blue-collar attitudes there was similar support expressed for the virtues of owning or working in a small business. Participants endorsed the importance of "not having to take orders," of "being your own boss," and being "independent."

But their appreciation of small business was very different from the glorification of "free enterprise' or "the free market" extolled by conservatives. The participants sharply distinguished between their support for small business and their attitudes toward Wall Street or corporate America. They described large companies like Walmart, for example, as essentially predatory and exploitative, undermining local businesses and not serving as a positive force in the community. They felt equally negative toward the destructive policies of banks and the financial system.

Nor did their approval of small business automatically translate into support for conservative economic policies. As many opinion polls have shown, many white workers actually support a very substantial range of "progressive" economic views and measures. The participants in the focus groups approved of making corporate executives pay their fair share of taxes and requiring them to obey a range of rules and regulations about the environment and conditions of labor. In short, these culturally traditional workers could sound quite "progressive" rather than "conservative" on an array of economic issues.

2. The Military

While progressives often equate support for the military with ill-advised foreign interventions and the neo-imperial ambitions of conservatives like Dick Cheney, this is quite distinct from the basic approval and identification that white workers feel for the military as an institution. It is rarely understood that for working class people, a career in the military is widely seen as profoundly admirable because military service upholds and honors very deeply held and distinctly working class values: ruggedness and bravery, teamwork and group solidarity, loyalty and self-sacrifice. In the rest of American culture these virtues are given a much lower value than more middle class values like intellectual ability, acquisitiveness, ambition, competiveness and the achievement of material success. For high school educated young men and women who are often not "successful" in these latter terms, the armed forces provide them with the opportunity to be seen as role models and heroes to their parents, families, friends and communities. In the eyes of working class Americans, "our men and women in uniform" are in essence the most important "working class heroes."

The deep support and respect that exists for the military is most dramatically reflected in the overwhelming and deeply emotional support for the veterans of Iraq and Afghanistan that the focus groups consistently expressed, and the intense anger and dismay they felt over the many failures they observed to treat the veterans as they deserved. In the focus groups, veterans were without question seen as the most admirable group in society and the most deserving of support.

3. Religious Faith

The third pillar of white working class cultural traditionalism is the firm belief that the Bible teaches good values and that religion is a positive force in family life.

The conservative perversion of this view is theocracy—the belief that Christians should have the right to impose Bible-based morality and rules of behavior on everyone. But among the "common-sense," middle-of-the road-sector of the white working class, there is a widespread and much more tolerant version of Christian belief, based in a more open-minded and forgiving understanding of the message of Jesus Christ. Although many white workers attend evangelical churches and these are often viewed as pillars of the religious right, the popular stereotypes of white working class evangelicals are often far from accurate. As the extensive sociological study *Christian America: What Evangelicals Really Want* noted:

All evangelicals are often stereotyped as imperious, intolerant fanatical meddlers. Certainly there are some evangelicals who fit this stereotype. But when listened to on their own terms, many prove to hold a civil, tolerant and non-coercive view of the world around them...for every one evangelical opposed to pluralism there were others who voiced an equally strong commitment to freedom of choice and toleration of diversity.

The strong majority of the men in the focus groups reflected this relatively tolerant perspective rather than endorsing theocracy. But what they also strongly expressed was a sense that the basic Christian values with which they grew up were being actively discouraged by society. As some noted:

What about the Bible? Doesn't that have a place in America anymore?

Why don't Democrats talk about religion? Why don't they ever stand up for it?

It is important to note, however, that, unlike ideological conservatives, the white working class men in the Hart Research/Fair Deal focus groups did not place the blame for the decline in traditional values only on elitist liberals or the lack of religion in society. On the contrary, a surprisingly large portion of these participants' anger was directed at the destruction of traditional values that was being caused by the greed and social indifference of modern business.

When asked about what has made America worse and undermined traditional values, these men repeatedly cited the corrupting effect on their children of cell phones, social media, movies and television, the fashion industry and the internet. They saw these technologies as deeply destructive, making their pre-teenage girls behave like "sluts," and their sons sneer at their father's values. They expressed a genuine fury at the loss of control over their children's lives. *"There aren't any casual 'pick up' sports games in the neighborhood like there were in my day,"* they complained. *"Kids just come home and disappear into their rooms to play videogames and stare at their computers."* It is not "liberals" who have done this, in their view; it is the result of an economy and culture where profitability and market share have become the only goal.

The men in these focus groups also perceive the culture created by the major media companies as culpable for the polarization of national political life. A number of participants in the focus groups faulted the media in particular for continually exaggerating and sensationalizing incidents of racial conflict. The media, they assert, blows up every divisive incident that occurs or gives wildly disproportionate coverage to peripheral issues like bathroom access for transgender individuals. *"Is this really the most important problem in America?"* one asked.

It was not the substance of these particular issues that these men necessarily objected to; it was the massive, disproportionate morning-to-night discussion of issues like these that they felt had little relevance to their lives. They were acutely aware that the TV stations were promoting these topics simply because they produced high ratings and internet "page views," not because the executives genuinely believed that these were really the most important social issues facing the country.

II. "Common sense, middle of the road" white workers do indeed respect and endorse core traditional cultural values, but they also endorse a more unexpected social value—a deep and genuine belief in "tolerance."

During the various focus groups, some of the outside observers of the sessions were genuinely surprised by the spontaneous expressions of tolerance that emerged during the discussions. Their surprise was understandable. "Working class whites" are so often equated with Trump supporters or hard-core ideological conservatives that hearing such views seemed quite incongruous.

But anyone who actually spends time with middle of the road white working class people knows that this is not unusual at all—indeed, it's quite common. This should not be a surprise. If a person is willing to try to *"see both sides"* of an issue or view questions with a *"on the one hand, on the other hand"* mode of thought, the necessary psychological result has to be a willingness to accept that even if one has strong personal convictions, other points of view can and should be treated with respect as well.

In the focus groups tolerant attitudes appeared again and again. Workers expressed *"live and let live"* attitudes about a wide range of issues connected to privacy, choice and freedom. Various participants insisted that they *"don't want to try to run other people's lives."* They were willing to accept a wide range of behavior that they personally might object to as long as it did not impinge on their own choices and way of life.

This was not some rare exception. One need only look at the wide range of issues on which the *"on the one hand on the other hand"* mode of thought appears in the sentences below, sentences fundamentally built around the word "but," as the basis for reaching tolerant conclusions.

> Politics: *"I may agree with the GOP on 90% of social issues ... **but** that doesn't mean I want to impose my views on everyone."*

Religion: *"I think we need to let religion back in schools… "**but** I'm not trying to push religion on anyone"*

Health care: *"I'm not for socialized medicine ….**but** we must help people in need."*

Immigration: *"I'm not saying nobody can come in to our country because that's not America….. **but** to come in and not pay any taxes, that's crazy."*

Gay Marriage: *"In 100 years I'll never understand what a man can see in another man…. **but** I got a friend in an interracial relationship and I think that's a good thing so who am I to be the judge of what someone else decides to do."*

Again and again the basic *"on the one hand but on the other hand"* way of thinking that is revealed in the use of the word *"**but**"* reappears. It is not occasional; it is common. Modern life exposes many white working people to diversity: the interracial couple who move in down the street, the gay guy who handles the bookkeeping for the trucking company where they work. Twenty or 30 years ago these kinds of personal experiences were rare in white working class life; now they are routine and workers have gradually adapted to the change.

Perhaps most dramatically, this even extends to attitudes about the emotional subject of race.

White workers in the groups very unselfconsciously expressed an "old fashioned" *"I have a dream"* philosophy about race—a philosophy that is now often viewed by progressives as naïve. They sincerely stated that they judge people by their character, not by the color of their skin. Participants indicated that they know some "good" African-Americans and some undesirable ones as well and they feel no embarrassment in categorizing African-Americans in this way. They express the same perspective regarding immigrants. They know one Mexican co-worker who is a "fine family man" and another who is "trouble" or "a bad dude." They do not share the liberal view that categorizing non-whites in this way represents a perpetuation of stereotypes or reflects an unconscious racism. They believe that they judge white people according to the same standards they use for non-whites and consider themselves entirely admirable because they choose to view and treat people in this "color-blind" way.

Some progressives believe that statements of this kind are simply a smoke-screen for an underlying racism and that unless a white person explicitly recognizes the reality of systemic racism and acknowledges his or her own position as the beneficiary of "white privilege," statements that "I judge people as individuals" represent little more than rationalizations to justify racial bias. In fact, some will even argue that whites who express overt bigotry are preferable because they admit their bias rather than concealing it.

A vast number of commentaries have been written regarding this debate, but when it is viewed from the specific perspective of Democratic political strategy one fact is inescapable: virtually no overt racists are going to vote for Democratic candidates, while some white workers who hold this "I judge people as individuals" view can, in fact, be convinced to vote Democratic. Categorizing all white workers who hold this "I judge people as individuals" view as essentially indistinguishable from overt racists unavoidably represents a decision to abandon these potentially winnable voters to the GOP.

 In the focus group sessions the important difference between this perspective and explicit racism emerged most dramatically in regard to the videos of police mistreatment or the unjustified shooting of African-Americans. Unlike the reflexive "support the police" attitudes racists and firm conservatives will usually express, these white working class men very firmly agreed that in some cases the video clearly showed that the policeman was totally wrong and his conduct utterly inexcusable and indeed criminal. Their only objection was that this should not automatically be assumed to always be the case and that all policemen and women should not be blamed for the actions of a minority.

III. In an ironic twist the admirable trait of common sense, middle of the road white working class support for tolerance becomes also a demand that liberals should be tolerant themselves and respect white working class values as well.

The flip side of "common sense," middle of the road workers support for tolerance, however, is a demand for respect for their own choices, lifestyle and views. The men in the focus groups felt that the traditional values they were taught as children are good values and deserve respect. They deeply value core elements of traditional working class culture like religious faith, patriotism and individual responsibility and they do not accept the view that such values should be treated as inherently ignorant or reactionary. In fact, it is this dismissal of their values and culture that produces the greatest antagonism toward Democrats and progressives.

This feeling is expressed most clearly in disgust with "political correctness," which they see as attempt to impose upon them values with which they do not agree. Unlike conservatives, a number of participants in the groups admitted that over the years they had gradually come to recognize that the biased cultural attitudes regarding African Americans that they'd held in the past were wrong and needed to be changed. They expressed sincere embarrassment at their previous views and felt pride at the way their views had evolved. But they simply would not accept that people who have no respect for the positive aspects of their culture should have the right to enforce upon them a whole range of rules and standards of behavior derived from a very different culture and social world.

Consider a few of the comments in the focus groups:

> *America used to be a melting pot and that's good but previous generations had to integrate, but now we're so PC we can't demand that any more. We get in trouble if we even raise the idea.*

> *Let's face it; you're automatically the bad guy if you complain about this stuff.*

> *Just because I don't agree with gay marriage doesn't mean I hate gays.*

> *We've all run out of white guilt.*

> *You shouldn't have to worry about everything you say.*

> *I really could care less what you do in your backyard but don't tell me what I have to do and believe in my backyard…freedom of speech….you're supposed to be able to think and say what you want in America but they want to force you to believe this and agree with that. No, I don't have to agree with everything you say.*

Liberals may disagree with these sentiments, but it is foolish to believe that they are no different from intolerant assertions that demand support for conservative ideology.

The most deeply and personally felt issue for a number of the participants in the focus groups was the imposition of what they felt to be political correctness on the job. More than a few participants noted that, *"people get fired and penalized over some little comment that should not be a big deal."* When several observers of the focus groups heard these statements they dismissed them as exaggerations and viewed them as essentially a rationalization for tolerating racial or gender insensitivity.

A number of participants in the sessions, however, reported direct personal experiences with friends or acquaintances who did indeed suffer real on-the-job consequences in such situations. The fact is often forgotten that in modern working class job sites like restaurants and other places where workers interact with customers, many lower level workers no longer have any form of job security whatsoever. In such places, even relatively minor customer complaints or dissatisfaction can very easily lead to a worker's demotion or dismissal without any recourse.

There is a deep irony here. In the union workplaces of the past, Democrats were proud to support the idea that a union shop steward should be available to defend an average worker from arbitrary dismissal if the employer was not able to demonstrate adequate cause. A worker was assumed to have the right to representation and an accusation of "bad behavior" would have to be arbitrated, not unilaterally and summarily decided by the boss.

Today, however, few workers have such protections and consequently feel vastly more vulnerable whenever a customer complains. The former sense of reasonable job security workers once felt has been eliminated in the new economy and workers have not failed to notice that their former defenders display no sympathy or even recognition of the change. It is an odd situation when liberals have no objection to arbitrary termination and assumed guilt for the worker in worker-employer disputes if the charge happens to be racial or gender insensitivity. If there were unions in such workplaces, defending workers from arbitrary dismissal with Democratic support, Democrats would not be so universally viewed as being indifferent to white working class concerns in this regard.

It is important to pause at this point and note a key fact. The three major psychological elements of middle of the road white workers' perspective—cultural traditionalism, support for tolerance and demand for respect for their own culture—are not independent psychological traits that can be mixed and matched like LEGO blocks. They form a mutually reinforcing mental framework that emerges from the basic "open-minded" mode of cognition that these men employ. Their respect for their own culture and views and their willingness to be tolerant of other perspectives are interrelated. Progressives cannot assume that they can detach white workers' displays of tolerance—of which they approve—from these workers' cultural traditionalism—of which progressives do not approve and wish they would discard. "Common sense" middle of the road white workers' basic mental frameworks cannot be taken apart and reassembled at will.

IV. "Common sense" middle of the road white workers don't see politicians as divided into left or right. They see them as all part of a single corrupt and parasitic new ruling class. Their hostility constitutes a modern form of class consciousness.

White working class ideological conservatives view politics and politicians through a strictly ideological lens. They believe that government is inherently evil and they sharply divide politicians into those they agree with—those who want to make government "small enough to drown in a bathtub," as conservative activist Grover Norquist once put it—and those they disagree with -- progressives who think government plays a positive and vital role in modern life.

The white workers in the focus groups, on the other hand, expressed a very different perspective.

In their comments they described politicians not simply as sometimes individually corrupt but as part of an inherently and irredeemably corrupt system that requires politicians to sell themselves to special interest contributors in order to get elected, and who inevitably use their position to become wealthy. They further perceive all politicians as living in an insular and elite artificial world of wealth and influence-peddling.

This view is not new. In their 1995 book, *Congress as Public Enemy*, political scientists John Hibbing and Elizabeth Theis-Morse described the views of the participants in their focus groups as follows:

> The American people have come to believe that the political system is run by a powerful professional political class (cut off from ordinary people) and that votes no longer make much difference because money rules...people believe that the Washington system runs on greed and special privilege.

They noted, in fact, that this perception was so strong that it represented "a new form of class consciousness."

In fact, the continuity and connection between this view and the class consciousness of the previous 1930's trade union era can be seen in the fact that for most white working class Americans the popular Roosevelt-era caricature of the immoral, top hatted millionaire, swilling champagne while orphans starved has been completely replaced by the modern vision of the venal and corrupt politician, making back room deals with cynical lobbyists in return for fat campaign contributions.

Stan Greenberg's organization Democracy Corps has conducted the most sustained and extensive polling research to study white working class attitudes about systemic political corruption. The polling data Democracy Corps has accumulated on this subject now includes tens of thousands of respondents.

In 2015, in the Second White Working Class Roundtable, Greenberg expressed his conclusions as follows:

> White working class voters … are open to an expansive Democratic economic agenda—to more benefits for child care and higher education, to tax hikes on the wealthy, to investment in infrastructure spending, and to economic policies that lead employers to boost salaries for middle- and working-class Americans, especially women. Yet they are only ready to listen when they think that Democrats understand their deeply held belief that politics has been corrupted and government has failed. Championing reform of government and the political process is the price of admission with these voters.

In the Hart Research/Fair Deal Project focus groups this uniformly cynical view was expressed again and again:

> *"They [politicians] all come out millionaires."*

> *"The majority of politicians have sold their soul for the almighty dollar."*

> *"Everybody that's in the government is a lawyer. They are from very well-to-do families. They've always had everyone doing things for them, and they're silver spoon in the mouth kind of people. They don't understand the little people like average Americans because they're not average Americans so they don't see the real problems."*

It is this intense categorical distrust and contempt for politicians and the political system as a whole that explains one of the most enduring frustrations progressives encounter in dealing with white working class people. For 40 years polls have repeated shown that majorities of white working people support a quite substantial range of basically progressive economic policies but, oddly, never vote for the Democratic politicians who promise to enact them.

The mystery disappears when it is understood that white working people tend to see Democrats as just as corrupted by the political system as GOP. Measures that Democrats themselves consider entirely altruistic policies to help not only the poor and needy but white working class people as well are seen by white workers as cynical electoral bribery to buy mostly minority votes. The pervasive cynicism gives Democrats absolutely no credit at all for altruism.

In consequence, white workers refuse to believe that even programs that appear to be in their direct self interest will actually work as promised. Instead they assume that such programs will be undermined by corruption and vote buying. They do not believe the promised benefits will ever "trickle down" to them.

As Guy Molyneux said in his American Prospect analysis of this same focus group data:

These voters agree that the economic system is "rigged" as populists like Senators Elizabeth Warren and Bernie Sanders like to say, but with a crucial difference. It is rigged not only to the advantage of those at the top. The men in the focus groups complain that the rich and the poor get taken care of today, while those in the middle get left behind.

This view was perfectly summarized by one participant who said: *"the left cares about the poor, the Right cares about the rich. Nobody cares about us."*

Regarding the poor and minorities, there is a combination of genuine concern and willingness to help those who are genuinely in need, along with an intense fury and contempt for the lazy, the dishonest and the criminal.

The participants expressed this dichotomy in many ways:

If you're in a wheelchair yeah, we'll help you. But if you're able bodied there no reason you're not working.

My mom is 70 years old. She has congestive heart failure. She has all kinds of health problems. She cannot work. She has not been able to work for 15 years ...so yeah she lives off $900 a month in assistance. She gets $16 in food stamps. But I have a friend who has never worked a day in her life but has five kids and also gets $900 a month in food stamps. That is not fair.

When conservatives express broad generalizations about "welfare queens and Cadillacs," it is reasonable for progressives to dismiss such statements as urban legends that mask simple prejudice. But the anecdotes offered in the focus groups were entirely different; they were highly detailed and specific stories of people - white people - that the participants knew personally, and who were frequently their own white neighbors and relatives. It was, in fact, precisely the very clear, detailed and vivid personal knowledge they demonstrated about such people taking advantage of the system that formed the basis for their intense anger.

This same distinction between fairness and unfairness also appeared in the participants' attitudes toward the wealthy. On the one hand, there was no antagonism for people who become wealthy through business success and virtually no support for abstract "income redistribution" or punitively taxing the rich as a matter of basic social justice. But at the same time there was a deep anger at the way the wealthy manipulated the system to pay lower taxes than ordinary workers or otherwise game the system to their advantage.

There was also a feeling that the rich had become increasingly separated from and indifferent to those below. As one participant stated *"They all live in gated communities these days and don't serve in military. They don't care about us and are happy to export our jobs all over the world.*

What kind of candidates will "common sense" middle of the road white workers support?

The focus group participants were directly asked to list the characteristics they most wanted in a political candidate. The results revealed a very striking fact. While white workers who are ideological conservatives will predictably respond to questions like this by listing a wide range of conservative policies they would want a candidate to support, the middle of the road participants in the groups responded in a very different way. What they most deeply and indeed passionately wished for were candidates with sound moral and ethical character, and a genuine commitment to the people they represent. Because they perceive all modern American politicians as corrupt, self-seeking parasites, the attributes they hope for in candidates are strong personal virtues like honesty, integrity and authenticity.

The range and intensity of the feelings that were expressed are startling:

Regarding greed and money, the kind of candidates they wanted were men and women who

See politics as public service, not a way to make money.

Focus on the needs of the people and not the special interests.

Care about the people of the country instead of just making their wallets bigger.

Are motivated by the needs of everyday citizens and not the high-dollar contributors.

Are not bought or corrupt.

Don't make getting rich their guiding principle.

The participants in the groups also wanted men and women who would be authentic, grass roots representatives of the communities that elected them. They said that "We need politicians".

Who know real people".

Who live in the community they represent.

Who have walked the walk and understand Americans' struggles.

Who remember where they came from and the people they represent.

Who have worked their way up by themselves without family and friends who got them where they are.

Who can be judged by their works, by what they have done in the past".

Who live their ethics in their own lives.

Who should be honest and want to represent the voice of the people.

The participants supplemented these general views with specific ideas: that candidates should live on their government salary and reject all other income; that they should come from and live in the very specific community that elected them.

The participants also reaffirmed the basic values that the candidates they wanted to support should personally embody: to defend traditional cultural values but at the same time to display tolerance and compassion for others.

It is important to notice that this distinctive, personal-character-based set of criteria describe a candidate who is profoundly different from many of the "blue dog" Democrats that progressives quite reasonably scorn. Such candidates pander to conservative hot button issues in order to win votes, while at the same time do not seriously defend workers' economic interests but rather take money from special interests and make no effort to reduce the influence of big money in politics.

The kind of candidate the common sense, middle of the road workers are describing is very different—a candidate who upholds core traditional values but very emphatically does not compromise with intolerance, and who rejects the corrupt big money system of modern political life.

The Implications for Democratic Strategy

In order to evaluate the implications of common sense, middle of the road white workers for Democratic strategy the first step that needs to be taken is to clearly distinguish between presidential and state-wide elections for senate and governorships, on the one hand, and elections for more local political offices on the other. In presidential elections and in many large, demographically diverse states with high percentages of both minorities and college-educated voters, a Democratic candidates' strategy will necessarily involve building a diverse coalition that may only require the support of a relatively small percentage of white working class voters. In these elections Democrats can often hope to win sufficient white working class votes simply by choosing more attractive candidates than were offered in 2016 or gambling that the economy turns sour.

At the level of congressional districts and other more local elections on the other hand, the GOP now routinely wins elections for a vast range of offices in significant measure by winning the support of very substantial majorities of white working class voters. The GOP dominance among these voters then gives them control of state governments and the House of Representatives, resulting in a conservative "veto power" over all social reform. To contest this dominance Democrats must run campaigns in many districts where white working people are the largest single group in the electorate.

On the surface the identification of a distinct middle of the road sector of the white working class would seem like an entirely positive finding for Democratic candidates, since it offers a promising audience for progressive and Democratic appeals. As the preceding sections have shown, these voters are substantially more tolerant than are firm Republicans, they are strongly hostile to the modern "big money" system of politics, and they hold relatively progressive or "populist" views on a significant range of economic issues. In 2012, 36 percent of white working class voters voted for Barack Obama according to the exit polls— 8 percent more than Hillary Clinton received in 2016—and 40 percent voted for Obama in the anti-GOP wave election of 2008. It would therefore seem that some segment of the 72 percent of white workers who voted for Trump this year should be open to Democratic appeals.

But the same analysis provided above also shows that there will be a very substantial sector of these middle of the road white workers who will simply refuse to consider voting for Democrats. The reality is that the kinds of candidates who can effectively appeal to these voters will tend to have two important characteristics that will limit Democratic inroads with the group.

First, candidates who will be able to successfully appeal to middle of the road white workers will tend to firmly assert and embrace key traditional values. They may endorse common sense gun regulations but they will also categorically support the rights of citizens to own guns. They will reject the notion that America should impose Christianity on all Americans, but they will equally firmly assert that Christian faith is a positive force in many Americans' family life, including their own. They will support a variety of populist measures but at the same time they will firmly endorse the virtues of small business and individual initiative.

Second, they will tend to clearly embody white workers' culture and values in their own personal life. Many will attend church on Sunday, others will have served in the military or have a background in a working class occupation or as the owner of a small or medium sized business. Many will go hunting on fall weekends, listen to country music in their car and be able to talk with first-hand knowledge and personal experience about the day to day problems of the white working class people in the neighborhoods and communities that they represent.

This presents two major problems for Democratic candidates. First, a very significant group of Obama coalition base voters will simply not feel comfortable supporting candidates of this kind. Like any other voters they will prefer to support a candidate who clearly reflects and embodies their own culture and values rather than the culture and values of white working class America. Many, in fact, will insist on firm liberal "litmus tests" for candidates and reject those who refuse to endorse specific pieces of progressive legislation or positions on issues.

At the same time, many middle of the road white workers will resist voting for a Democratic candidate who seems to them to represent a variety of groups other than their own and who appears to see white working people as only one part of a disparate coalition. This was the most intense and passionate objection the participants in the focus groups had with Democrats—the sense that Dems cared more about other groups in the Democratic coalition than they did about them or that Dems were cynical political deal-makers who distributed government favors to different groups in return for votes.

Democrats have, of course, traditionally believed that offering social and economic policies and programs that objectively serve white workers' real interests should be able to overcome such objections but this ignores the profound importance that not just white working class voters but all voters place on having a candidate who genuinely *represents* them. Surveys have revealed that a major element of Trump's appeal to white working class voters was not his specific positions on issues but rather his assertion that "I'm your guy" -- that he was running to represent them and not anyone else. The reality is that a Democratic candidate who cannot convincingly project this sense of being a genuine, deeply passionate representative of white workers will simply not be able to win their widespread support.

As a result, the "common sense" middle of the road sector of the white working class must therefore be seen as divided into two distinct groups— those who can be convinced to support Democratic candidates and those who are alienated from the GOP but will simply not vote for Democrats.

In order to more clearly define the divisions within white working class America, it is worthwhile to replace the basic three-part division used in Democratic political campaigns between firm supporters, firm opponents and persuadable voters with a larger four-part framework:

I. Absolutely Firm GOP/Trump partisans	II. Common Sense, Middle of the Road Voters—	III. Common Sense, Middle of the Road Voters—	IV. Firm Democrats— Voted Democratic in 2016
	Not firm GOP partisans but will refuse to vote for Democrats	Persuadable (8% of white working class voters supported Obama in 2012 and 12% in 2008 but then did not vote for Hillary in 2016)	
Key activist base groups: (a) racists/white supremacists (b) Ideological conservatives (c) Religious right			
????	????	8-12%	28%

There is no reliable research right now on the exact relative size of these groups but the problem that leaps out from this chart is the group in section II—those who are not firm GOP partisans but who will also refuse to vote for Democrats. Based on their voting patterns in recent elections, this second "will not vote for Democrats" group is very likely to represent a significantly larger segment of the white working class than the sector that is potentially open to Democratic appeals.

Thinking "outside the box" of traditional Progressive / Democratic strategy

In conventional political strategy it would therefore seem that, unfortunate as it may be, these voters should simply be ignored. But this is a deeply disturbing choice because it inherently abandons these voters to add their votes to the GOP. The alternative, on the other hand, is to step back and to think outside the default framework of progressive strategy—that the only strategic objective worth pursuing is the election of Democratic candidates. This should indeed be the primary objective whenever possible, but, particularly at this critical time, it should not be considered the only conceivable goal.

One thing that became clear in the focus groups described in the analysis above was the deep desire of the common sense, middle of the road white working class voters to vote for candidates who genuinely reflect their values and views—even if such candidates had no realistic chance of winning. A large proportion of common sense, middle of the road workers are profoundly disgusted with both political parties and the big money system in political life. Many would appreciate the opportunity to express their position with a protest vote for an independent candidate, even if the result might be that a Democratic candidate would defeat a Republican.

What this means is that candidates who choose to authentically represent "common sense" middle of the road workers could gain significant white working class support if they ran as grass-roots independents, with the inevitable consequence of splitting and weakening the dominant extremist wing of the GOP. These candidates could turn their lack of "big money" financing into an advantage by attacking their opponents for being partic-ipants in the corrupt system of big money campaigns. Moreover, as Trump has demonstrated, unique and unusual "populist" candidates can garner substantial free media coverage if their message is new and dramatic.

Granted, even with these strategies, raising sufficient money would present a major challenge. In the dramatically new level of political involvement that has emerged since the 2016 election, however, the possibility of significant small donor financing for independent candidates is no longer beyond the realm of possibility

The possible emergence of independent middle of the road white working class candidates is vitally important today. Any initiative that divides today's dominant GOP coalition must be seen as a vital objective for progressive and Democratic strategy.

The current political situation has become profoundly dangerous precisely because Donald Trump has attracted an additional layer of often passionate support from many white working people with an appeal that bears a recognizable similarity to the program and agenda of the European National Socialist and Fascist Parties of the 1930's and which resembles the appeal of the neo-fascist French National Front today. It is an appeal based on scapegoating and demonizing minorities, promoting a belligerent nationalism and offering demagogic promises of massive public works projects and restoration of high wage jobs in factories and mines. It is because of this new level of support from Trump voters that the GOP coalition has now gained complete control of all three branches of government, posing an unprecedented threat to America.

There are a vast number of white working class communities in America where the GOP wins overwhelming "supermajorities"— where Democratic organization is literally non-existent and Democratic candidates are simply not considered a serious alternative. In these communities political competition is not a debate between liberal and conservative views but a competition among Republicans for who can claim the title of the "real conservative."

In these communities where a meaningful Democratic alternative does not really exist, the emergence of independent "common sense middle of the road" candidates who challenged this conservative consensus would be a highly positive development - particularly because in the future, Republican candidates who appeal to white working class voters are almost surely going to incorporate Donald Trump's vicious white supremacist rhetoric and agenda into their campaigns. Independent middle of the road campaigns would break the apparent ideological consensus that conservative views now enjoy.

Even in predominantly white working class communities where a larger segment of the common sense, middle of the road white workers might be open to Democratic candidates the simultaneous emergence of grass roots independent candidates would in many cases still be a net benefit to Democrats. Such candidates would tend to draw more support from Republicans than Democrats, providing a net benefit to the latter.

This would also be true in demographically diverse districts where Democratic candidates only have a chance of victory if they can win the strong support of all the other sectors of the existing Democratic coalition and just a relatively small minority of white working class votes. Because it would split the GOP vote, a three-way race that included an independent candidate would still provide a greater opportunity for the Democrat to win a plurality than a two-way race against a Republican would provide the opportunity for winning an outright Democratic majority.

The GOP has won its current hegemonic position in white working class America by uniting right-wing and more moderate white workers under the umbrella of "the real America" and convincing them that the only alternative to the GOP is distant and indifferent coastal liberal elites. The development of independent common sense candidates could undermine this strategy and isolate the racially prejudiced and staunchly conservative right wing of the GOP as a minority group in white working class America. Given the unprecedented threat posed by Donald Trump's success among white working class voters, this would be a development of tremendous importance that progressives and Democrats would clearly recognize as distinctly positive.

(Endnotes)
1. Internal memo, Working America

2. http://prospect.org/article/mapping-white-working-class

3. ibid

4. For an extended discussion of this concept, see Chapters 5 and 6 of Levison, *The White Working Class Today: Who They Are, How They Think and How Progressives Can Regain Their Support*

5. Christian Smith, Christian America: What Evangelicals Really Want, Santa Barbara, University of California Press, 2002

6. John Hibbing and Elizabeth Theiss-Morse, Congress As Public Enemy, London, Cambridge University Press, 1994

THE OUTLOOK FOR 2018 AND 2020
Ed Kilgore

The basic political context for the discussion about white working class voters is the urgent challenge of the 2018 and 2020 elections. These elections will determine whether the horrendous outcome of the 2016 elections represented a wakeup call for progressives, or a nightmare that has only just begun. If Democrats do not make significant gains in the states in these two elections, Republicans will dominate another decennial round of redistricting that could place not only state legislatures but also the U.S. House out of reach until 2032. The odds of Republicans earning a "lock" on the House go up even more if Democrats don't win a significant number of seats in the midterms and the next presidential year.

Worse yet, if Republicans maintain "trifecta" control of the federal government beyond 2020, they will almost certainly impose policies on the country whose implications are difficult to project, but that transcend any present slicing and dicing

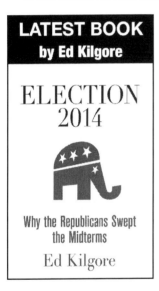

LATEST BOOK
by Ed Kilgore

ELECTION 2014

Why the Republicans Swept the Midterms

Ed Kilgore

Also By Ed Kilgore

New York Magazine commentator Ed Kilgore presents an overview of 30 congressional seats that Democrats are targeting in 2018. As he says:

The expected postelection "struggle for the soul" of the Democratic Party has now been replaced by optimism. "Tsunami" elections like those Democrats are hoping for in 2018 often build slowly. But across the country anti-Trump activists believe they can see big waves gathering.

http://nymag.com/daily/intelligencer/2017/04/what-democrats-need-to-do-to-take-congress-in-2018.html

Ed Kilgore is a Commentator for New York Magazine and a Co-Director of the White Working Class Roundtable

of the electorate. Winning back a significant share of the white working class vote at some future juncture may come too late if the New Deal policies that once made them vote for Democrats have been consigned to the dustbin of history.

So the specific challenges of 2018 and 2020 need to be at the front of every progressive's mind in considering the long-term regeneration of our electoral coalition.

2018: Finally, Democrats may have a midterm cycle they can win.

Fortunately, Democrats should have a decent environment for making gains in the U.S. House and many gubernatorial and legislative elections in 2018. Unfortunately, that environment probably will not extend to the U.S. Senate. (More about that later.)

Normally the party controlling the White House loses support in midterms, and in presidential reelection years makes gains or more or less stands pat.

Looking at recent midterms, in U.S. House races the presidential party lost 31 seats in 2006, 63 in 2010 and 13 in 2014. Not counting special elections, Democrats will need to win 24 seats in 2018 to gain control of the chamber.

In U.S. Senate races the White House party lost six seats in 2006, six in 2010 and nine in 2014. Democrats would need a net gain of just three seats in 2018 to regain the control they lost in 2014.

In governorships, it lost six in 2006, six in 2010, and three in 2014.

Translated to popular votes, the presidential partly lost (as measured by the national House vote) by 8 per cent in 2006, 7 per cent in 2010 and 6 percent in 2014. Thanks to the impressive job of gerrymandering Republicans executed prior to 2012, Democrats would probably need to win the House popular vote by somewhere between 7 and 12 percent to give Nancy Pelosi back her gavel as Speaker. It's possible but hardly easy.

A substantial degree of pessimism regarding Democratic prospects in the Senate is necessary because the party faces one of the worst landscapes in recent history. Democrats must defend 25 of the 35 seats at stake. Eleven of those 25 are in states carried by Trump in 2016; only one Republican (Dean Heller of NV) is in a state carried by Hillary Clinton. Nine of the seats that Democrats must defend are in states that combine, unfortunately, a high percentage of non-college educated white voters and a low percentage of minority voters—a combination that made them so hospitable to Trump. In the initial Cook Political Report Senate ratings for 2018, only two Republican seats are anything less than "Solid R," while 13 Democratic seats are less than "Solid D." This does not mean Democrats will necessarily lose seats, but it does mean winning the net three needed to regain the chamber would take a genuine tsunami and some strokes of luck as well.

In fact, because the Senate landscape is so bleak, Democratic success or failure among white working class voters may not have an impact on control of the upper chamber in 2018. But success could sure do wonders for Democratic Senators who must defend their seats next year: Bob Casey, Joe Manchin, Sherrod Brown, Joe Donnelly, Claire McCaskill, Debbie Stabenow, Heidi Heitkamp and Tammy Baldwin, all of whom hail from states Trump carried that have relatively high percentages of non-college educated white voters. And while gaining seats will be difficult, minimizing losses to give Democrats a chance at regaining control in 2020 or 2022 could be crucial down the road.

Class and Race in 2018

The 2018 picture for the House is immensely complicated, but it helps to understand that the racial and educational cleavages that were so important to the 2016 presidential election are crucial to the House landscape as well. A comprehensive demographic analysis of House districts by Ron Brownstein and Leah Askarinam provides some useful signposts:

> From the presidency through lower-ballot races, Republicans rely on a preponderantly white coalition that is strongest among whites without a college degree and those living outside of major metropolitan areas. Democrats depend on a heavily urbanized (and often post-industrial) upstairs-downstairs coalition of minorities, many of them clustered in lower-income inner-city districts. They also rely on more affluent college-educated whites both in cities and inner suburbs.

Tellingly, Brownstein and Askarinam suggest that the presidential patterns in 2016 are actually converging with what we've been seeing in House races and were not some sort of anomaly attributable to the distinctive characteristics of the presidential candidates. Unfortunately, they note that Republicans have a congressional significant advantage:

> [W]hites exceed their share of the national population in 259 seats, and Republicans hold fully 196 of those—which puts them on the brink of a congressional majority even before they begin to compete for the more diverse seats. And there are 244 districts where the white share of college graduates lags the national average, and Republicans hold 176 of those. (Most of them overlap with the districts where the number of minorities is also fewer than average.)

Indeed, the Republican majority in the House now depends very heavily on overwhelming strength in the 176 districts with both low diversity and low levels of college education.

> Back in 2009, when the Democratic caucus still featured a large number of rural, culturally conservative "blue dogs"—like John Tanner of Tennessee, Ike Skelton o Missouri, and John Spratt of South Carolina—Republicans held a modest 20-seat advantage in these districts. After the 2010 election, the GOP exploded their lead in the low-diversity, low-education districts to 90 seats. The gap widened again to 125 seats in 2014, and edged up to 128 after 2016. The Republican success in hunting the blue dogs   nearly   to   extinction   presaged   the   big margins Trump marshaled from small places, particularly in interior states, to overcome Clinton's advantages in the largest urban centers.

It's doubtful that many of these "lo-lo" districts have a sufficiently large Democratic voting base to make a Democratic comeback possible, even if the party's performance among white working class voters improves significantly.

But Democrats have actually done better than they did in their last landslide victory year of 2008 in districts at the other end of the diversity/education spectrum:

Compared with the 111th Congress from early 2009 to early 2011, when Democrats last controlled the majority, the Democratic Party has actually widened its advantage in the districts high in both diversity and college-educated whites (from 50 seats then to 66 now). Since then, Democrats have lost ground modestly in the high-diversity districts with fewer-than-average white college graduates (from a 28-seat advantage to a 20-seat edge now). The party has also skidded somewhat more sharply in the districts with low diversity and large numbers of college-educated whites (from an advantage of 19 seats then to a deficit of five now).

The most obvious targets for each party in 2018 are House members in districts carried by the other party's presidential nominee in 2016. These districts also tend to be "stragglers behind enemy lines" in demographic terms, as Brownstein and Askarinam put it.

Twenty-three House Republicans won in districts carried by Hillary Clinton in 2016. Barack Obama only carried about a third of them in 2012. These districts are characterized in an analysis by Larry Sabato's Crystal Ball as having "higher-than-average numbers of college graduates and/ or are more diverse than the average district." Fifteen of them are in the Sunbelt, seven in California alone. There are other districts that Clinton narrowly lost, but made big gains over Obama's performance. One of them is GA-6, where a special election is being held to replace HHS Secretary Tom Price.

The districts represented by Democrats that were carried by Donald Trump, as one might expect, typically have less diversity and a less educated white population. Half are in the Midwest; three in Minnesota.

An improved performance among white working class voters would obviously help Democrats minimize their losses in these twelve potentially vulnerable districts, and could also be pivotal in what might be close races in the districts where the big push will be among higher-educated white voters. In the end, a vote is a vote, but while an exchange of "straggler" districts would give Democrats a net boost, it would not be enough to gain control of the chamber.

From a macro point of view, Democrats will struggle to win the House so long as their performance among white working class voters remains as disastrous as it was not only in 2016 (a 35-point loss), but in the midterms of 2010 and 2014 (both were 30-point losses). These voters do not vote at as high a rate as college-educated white voters in either presidential or midterm elections, but they represented 36 percent of the electorate as recently as 2014. Yes, they are declining as a percentage of the population, but not fast enough to make losses on the levels Democrats suffered in 2014 and 2016 sustainable without favorable shifts elsewhere.

The example of 2006

The ideal scenario for Democrats, as it happens, was in 2006, the last time Democrats were in the situation like the one they face today, running against a Republican president and Congress.

Political scientist Alan Abramowitz provides a reminder:

> At that time, there were only 18 Republican seats in districts carried by John Kerry in 2004, and Democrats had to defend 42 of their own seats in districts carried by George W. Bush. Nevertheless, Democrats were able to win back control of the House, making a net gain of 31 seats. In addition to winning 10 of the 18 Republican seats in districts carried by Kerry in 2004, Democrats won 20 Republican seats in districts carried by Bush and won an open seat previously held by then-Rep. Bernie Sanders (I-VT).

> The lesson of 2006 for Democratic strategists is not to focus exclusively on districts carried by Hillary Clinton but to cast their net considerably wider. In a midterm election with an unpopular president, the out- party can win a considerable number of seats in districts carried by the president's party in the previous election. In 2006, Democrats took back 10 of 41 Republican seats in districts in which George W. Bush won between 50percent and 55percent of the major-party vote and seven of 58 districts in which Bush won between 55percent and 60percent. They even captured three districts in which Bush won at least 60percent of the vote.

2006 also showed that losses for an incumbent president's party can mushroom when said president is especially unpopular. As Abramowitz notes, George's W. Bush's final Gallup approval rating before the 2006 midterms was 38 percent. Trump could well be in similar territory in 2018.

Amazingly, in 2006 Democrats actually carried the over-60 vote (albeit by an eyelash, after a failed GOP effort to privatize Social Security), and only lost white working class voters by ten points (they had lost this group by 20 points in 2004). Numbers anything like that would guarantee a Democratic wave, even if "Obama Coalition" voters don't turn out in huge numbers.

The X-factor in 2018 will be turnout patterns. A Trump presidency in alliance with a GOP Congress could be the one thing that diminishes or even reverses the midterm "falloff" in participation by two groups that have recently become central to the Democratic electorate: young and minority voters. This year's special and off-year elections could be a leading indicator of what might happen in the midterms.

2020—A Do or Die Year for Democrats

The incessant intra-Democratic arguments over the catastrophe of 2016 don't often pay enough attention to the future. But obviously a Democratic presidential win in 2020 is essential to avoid a catastrophic long-term decline of government as a positive force in national life. A GOP victory could produce a very conservative majority on the U.S. Supreme Court for decades to come; and (assuming Donald Trump or someone much like him is the GOP nominee) a Republican flirtation with serious authoritarianism and the massive disenfranchisement of Democratic voters. The very gradual demographic drift towards higher levels of Democratic-leaning demographic groups will inevitably continue, but just as in 2016, such trends cannot be relied on to produce victory.

The most plausible way to feel optimistic about the 2020 presidential race is to look at the positive popular vote totals from 2016, and the roughly 80,000-vote margin in three states that gave Trump his electoral college majority, and then to focus on simple ways to use party and candidate resources better to reverse this outcome. Certainly Democrats in 2020 are not likely to suffer from over-confidence, or from voters' misapprehension that Trump is free from corruption or corporate influence.

But down-ballot races in 2020 could be just as important as the top of the ticket. It will be a precious opportunity to create a governing "trifecta" by winning the White House and both Houses of Congress in one fell swoop. If as expected Democrats make gains in the House in 2018, another push in 2020 could get them over the top, particularly since presidential turnout patterns are normally more beneficent than midterms to Democrats. After the dreadful Senate landscape of 2018, Democratic will get a break in 2020, when two-thirds of the seats up are currently held by Republicans (though only two of them are in states carried by Hillary Clinton last November).

Perhaps most importantly, 2020 will be the final chance for state-level gains before the next decennial reapportionment and redistricting process kicks in. As with the U.S. House, the hope is that marginal gains in 2018 will be a springboard for improvements that bring Democrats near parity, especially in the states (e.g., Florida, Michigan, North Carolina, Ohio, Pennsylvania and Texas) where GOP gerrymandering has been so egregious in the recent past.

In terms of the white working class vote, improvements over the 2016 performance are to be expected, if only because four years of broken Trump promises to his supporters in this demographic group, along with favoritism towards the very elites he claims to despise, should have an impact if Democrats are minimally competent in publicizing these developments to working Americans.

If everything goes well for the Donkey Party in 2020, perhaps progressives will return once again to speculating about the sufficiency of youth and minority votes for the future. But even in that happy contingency, white working class voters will have a moral hold on Democrats that is just as important as their political value. It is to be profoundly hoped that Democrats never again need to be reminded of that fundamental fact as they were in 2016.

Made in the USA
Middletown, DE
03 August 2017